I Love You

FROM
THE

Edges

Lessons from Raising Grandchildren

KAREN BEST WRIGHT

authorHOUSE®

AuthorHouse™ LLC
1663 Liberty Drive
Bloomington, IN 47403
www.authorhouse.com
Phone: 1-800-839-8640

Author photo by Larry Lyon www.ldlyon.com

Portions of this book were published in slightly different form as "Being There for a Child Forever" in Wondrous Child: The Joys and Challenges of Grandparenting, edited by Lindy Hough, published by North Atlantic Books, 2012. Used by permission of the publisher."

Published by AuthorHouse 05/15/2014

ISBN: 978-1-4969-1183-4 (sc)
ISBN: 978-1-4969-1182-7 (hc)
ISBN: 978-1-4969-1181-0 (e)

Library of Congress Control Number: 2014908612

CONTENTS

ACKNOWLEDGEMENTS

Appreciation to my family and friends who encouraged me to write my story, especially to my daughters Jennifer, Melissa, and Angela who provided me with great emotional support over the past decade.

Appreciation to my daughter Kayla and her children. Without them I would have no such story to share. They have been a blessing in my life.

Acknowledgement of five of my terrific grandchildren Bella, Alex, Vincent, Layla, and Coulsen on the front cover of this book.

Appreciation to my friend, Phil Sisk, for the hours of reading and honest editing of my writings. He has been a steady support throughout the entire process.

Appreciation to Larry Lyon for taking my personal photo.

My love goes to all eight of my children who, through either loving me or challenging me, made me a better person, mother, and grandmother.

I am grateful to all of the grandparents who have written me and shared their stories with me over the past several years. They have shown unwavering love in regards to raising their grandchildren, love that keeps families together.

NAME DISCLOSURE

A few names in my story have been changed to protect individual privacy. Others chose to have their real names used. As one daughter stated, "You may use my real name. I trust you will write an authentic and loving story."

DEDICATION

This book is dedicated to all of the loving grandparents and relatives raising children in an effort to keep their families together. The depth of love that these relatives have for their family's children is honorable and amazing.

I Love You
from the Edges

A love story of raising my young granddaughters for several years, letting them capture my heart, my life, and my soul, and then having to give them back — resulting in a painful, yet spiritual journey of love, healing, and reunion.

INTRODUCTION

When I was raising three of my grandchildren, lurking beneath the surface, behind the façade of self-confidence and optimism, was the fear of *not* raising the children. While starting over with babies was not necessarily on my bucket list, it was something I welcomed with opened arms and a grateful heart.

I Love You from the Edges is more than my story of raising grandchildren. In Part One, I not only tell my own heart-felt experiences and memories of struggle, grief, and joy that spanned more than a decade, I also share stories from other grandparents and relative caregivers who openly shared their hearts with me. Reading about the experiences of other grandparents and relatives raising children may be very helpful to you when embarking on this same journey. Learning that you are not alone may help you feel supported and feel compassion from others. For the sake of simplicity, I use the word grandchildren or grandparent to represent all types of kinship relationships. So whether you are a grandparent, aunt, uncle, great-something, or sibling caring for children, this book is for you.

Part Two continues with the experiences of grandparents and relatives along with *know how* suggestions on *what to do* and *how to do it*. These suggestions include ideas on understanding the legal process, finding available resources, obtaining needed medical care, and what to expect when enrolling children in school. Since there are not sufficient resources to make this journey easy, and state laws and resources vary from state to state, I provide recommendations from those who have lived through it. A list of Internet resources (websites) that provide a wealth of information for relative caregivers is included, as well as suggestions on doing a general online search for needed information.

The Appendix concludes our journey with a copy of the Kinship Wellness Assessment and Goal Setting program that I developed. This assessment was inspired by my own need to create balance in my life. While completing my master's degree in Psychology: Specialization in Health & Wellness, I realized the importance of focusing on six aspects of wellness: physical, emotional, mental/intellectual, social, spiritual, and environmental. Through my contacts with other grandparents who were also raising grandchildren, I discovered that many also suffered from a lack of wellness and balance in their lives. I designed this program to help grandparents become aware of their own personal wellness needs and to set goals for self-improvement. Grandparents often neglect themselves in their efforts to take care of a young generation of children. We can only succeed if we also take care of ourselves as well. I continue to use the ideas in this program to help me assess my own ongoing needs in regards to all aspects of my own wellness. I excel in some areas and continue to struggle in others. The objective of the program is to bring awareness which can empower us to make healthier choices for ourselves.

PART ONE

CHAPTER 1

Twinkle, Twinkle Little Star

Summer, 2002: With only the youngest of my eight children still at home, I called my mother. The conversation went something like this: "Mother, I am so glad I still have Angela at home. I'm just not ready to not have children." I had always loved being a mother, even when all eight of my kids lived at home. Raising a large family had been a continual juggling act, but now I had the time and energy to be the *perfect* mother to one easy, sweet-natured teenager. Angela was just starting high school, so I had three years before facing the empty nest syndrome I preferred would never happen. In June of that year I remarried. With Angela at her father's for the summer, I was carefree with few concerns. I went dancing with my new husband, enjoyed site-seeing on his Harley, and settled into his home, all while doing a lot of reorganizing to make room for Angela and myself in his home. I was apprehensive about being in someone else's space, but it was a nice home and I was optimistic about our future.

Yet, change was in the air. I could feel it; I could smell it; I could almost touch it. Then in late August, my daughter Kayla gave birth in Texas to Grace who was premature and weighed only two pounds. I flew to Houston to help take care of siblings Myah, eighteen months old, and Lindsey, four years old, for a couple of weeks until I found ladies from a church group to help Kayla with the children. I will never forget the first time I saw Grace, sleeping in an incubator in the neonatal intensive care unit (NICU), hooked to tubes and by then weighing only 1 ½ lbs. Grace was fragile and looked breakable. I was afraid to even touch her

1

for fear of hurting her. "It's really not scary Mom," Kayla had said, as she gently reached in and touched Grace's hand. But every time I tried to touch the newborn treasure, I felt panic and couldn't breathe.

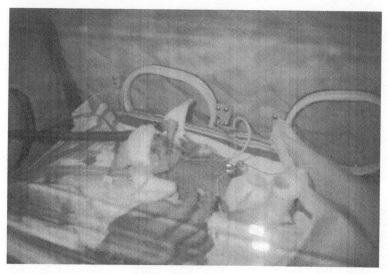

Newborn Grace

I had never seen such a tiny baby, so I just watched this most amazing twinkling little star who became a most precious diamond in my world. After two weeks, I returned home. Angela was starting a new high school and I was certain she needed her mother.

October, 2002: The simplicity of being a mother to one child was about to change. The phone rang; it was Kayla. The course of my life was about to change for the next several years. Due to unfortunate circumstances, Kayla needed my help with the girls. Grace was now two months old and finally ready to leave the hospital. I immediately left home and drove from Virginia to Texas and brought back with me three little granddaughters: Grace, almost five pounds and on a heart monitor, two-year-old Myah, and four-year-old Lindsey. Kayla, holding back the tears from a breaking heart, helped me load the children and their belongings into my car. Lindsey got off to a rough start. After we finished loading, Kayla headed back to her apartment, desperately needing to get out of sight. Lindsey insisted, "Mommy did not give me a bye kiss. I want a hug and a kiss. I want Mommy to give me a bye kiss." I assured Lindsey, "Your Mommy gave you kisses and hugs." She insisted she didn't get a bye kiss. I insisted she did. We could not have forgotten hugs and kisses. I felt certain we must have remembered the necessary and proper good-byes amidst the feeling of chaos. As I did not want to redo all of the painful good-byes, we started the drive with Lindsey in tears. Frequent stops were required to feed and change Grace, along with changing pull-ups for Myah and Lindsey. Myah spoke not a word the entire trip. In fact, I didn't even know she could already talk. She also did not cry at all. She was just eerily silent. I didn't quite know what to make of it. I did not know then that her total silence was the sign of a traumatized child. Meanwhile, Lindsey talked non-stop, repeating the same incomplete sentence about her daddy the entire three day trip. I didn't want to tell her to be quiet because I knew she was deeply traumatized. Even if I had tried to quiet her, I would not have succeeded in controlling her obsession with her daddy. We stopped frequently; and every time we did, it always took at least an hour, even just to get gas. After three long days of fast food, motels, and gas stations, my nerves were rattled as I pulled into my driveway, totally exhausted. However, the hard part had just begun; I had no idea how I was going to manage everything, but like other grandparents who faced the same situation, I did not hesitate. Kayla had been diligent in providing me with a power of attorney for the children, the children's birth certificates, and their social security cards. She wanted to make sure I had everything I needed to properly care for the children and to get all possible services that might be available for them.

The first year was the most difficult for everyone. Initially, I had to get the children signed up for Medicaid. Because we were grandparents, the children qualified for Medicaid. At least that was the case in Virginia. It was very important that I applied immediately, as the hospital in Houston would not even release Grace to me until they were certain that I had made a doctor's appointment for her. She needed to be seen immediately upon arriving at her new home. The first medical appointment was with our family practitioner, who was wonderful. This was followed by many appointments for Grace with a neonatologist, a pediatric cardiologist, and even with a pediatric ophthalmologist. Throughout a blistery cold winter, an infant carrier in my right hand and the heart monitor in my left, bundled up, I trudged from the house to the car, from the car to the hospital, and home again, sometimes with Lindsey and Myah in tow. Tucked away in the diaper bag was the power of attorney that gave me permission to do all of this. Eventually, I provided all medical providers with the legal custody papers; but until then, they accepted what I had. Feeding Grace every three hours 24/7 for a year took its toll, as I was going through menopause at the same time. Many nights I woke up to the *screaming* of the heart monitor. I would get up, make sure Grace was breathing properly, reset the monitor, change my nightgown because it was soaked from night sweats, and go back to sleep - until I needed to feed her again. Often I strapped the baby to me in a front infant sling and carried the monitor on my left shoulder as I took care of Myah and Lindsey. Even after the heart monitor was discontinued, Grace was often attached to me with the baby sling.

For obvious reasons, I was not sleeping well. When I did sleep, I had nightmares. I dreamt I was missing my plane, riding backwards on a bus, or was simply lost. I was exhausted. I had a hard time keeping up with my home-based business, which required extensive computer use, the normal tedious chores of housework, and helping the little ones adjust to a new life without their mother. This proved particularly difficult for Lindsey.

During one of Grace's visits to the pediatric cardiologist when she was about seven months old, I placed her on the patient bed and stepped back while the doctor listened to her heart. As I backed away, she started to cry. My instinct was to immediately reach for her, but I resisted and stood back. The doctor was actually pleased that she cried. *What? Maybe he was interested in the strength of her lungs.* I didn't know. I questioned his pleasure. "This is good to see," he explained. "Premature babies sometimes do not bond with their caregivers, even their own mothers, after having spent so much time in the hospital. It is obvious that she has developed a strong bond with you. I am glad to see that." I had not thought of that, but then I had never had a premature baby before.

After the first few months, Myah and Lindsey went to daycare, and Lindsey went two days a week to the public school Project 4 program (a pre-kindergarten program). I was fortunate to live in a county that provided daycare for grandparents who were raising grandchildren. Because the children qualified for Medicaid and a child-only TANF grant (Temporary Assistance for Needy Families), they also qualified for daycare. A child-only TANF grant is based on the children's income, not the grandparents. Since the children had no income, we qualified for a small monthly grant, along with daycare, Medicaid, and the Women, Infant, and Children (WIC) Supplemental Nutrition Program, which provided formula for the baby along with other healthy food for Myah and Lindsey. I later learned how fortunate we were as not all counties in Virginia provided daycare. Grace did not go to daycare; she stayed home with me until she was four because of a weak immune system. When she turned four, she started the public school's Project 4 program as Lindsey and Myah had done. Again, I was fortunate as not all counties in Virginia even had the Project 4 program. In fact, most didn't *(Additional possible resources are addressed in Part Two of this book).*

Becoming a full-time "mommy' to babies and toddlers had been natural for me when I had my own children, but I had never been a fifty-year-old menopausal woman with babies. Regardless of the colossal difficulties, I loved living with these little girls. They truly were my twinkling little stars as I rocked and sang to them daily, building an unbreakable bond between us. It did not take long for the girls to choose their favorite bedtime songs, usually the longest ones.

Six months after the children arrived in Virginia, we filed for custody. By law, the children needed to be in the state for six months before we could proceed. I wanted to make sure that Kayla was in a position to finish raising her children before I gave them back to her. Without a legal custody order there would be no assurance of that. I knew a simple Power of Attorney could be revoked at any time, and I had no legal rights as a grandparent, except those given to me by a judge. This move for custody upset Kayla terribly, as she believed I was over-reacting. I did not think I was, but then I often think I'm not over-reacting, even when I am. Kayla asked if I would agree to joint legal custody with her, while my husband and I had sole physical custody of the children. This meant that she had a right to be involved in all decision making with regard to the children, but they resided solely with us. I agreed. Visitation was also addressed and was set to be as agreed upon between us, as needs dictated and not as a carved in stone schedule. Even though it was not a complicated custody order, it still cost us thousands of dollars in legal fees and was a humiliating and hurtful experience for Kayla. Legally, everything seemed to proceed smoothly - until we clashed over the agreement a few years later.

During that first year, Kayla left Texas and asked to move in with us in Virginia. My husband and I, with the advice of our attorney, decided that she could not for two reason. First, my new marriage had become very complicated, and we lived in his house. And second, I was advised that all of the state and county assistance we received for the children would cease if their mother also lived with us. So, we said *no* and Kayla moved in with friends, four hours away. I have no doubt that, had I been single at the time, I would have handled this differently. Being within a workable, although not convenient, driving distance, Kayla was able to visit her children in our home, and we occasionally took them to her. It was not ideal, but we all dealt with it as best we knew how. Now, years later, my perspective on many things has changed. During those early years, it was hard to see clearly when I was smack in the middle of a constant crisis and living on adrenaline.

CHAPTER 2

Rub a dub, dub, 3 girls in a tub
And who do you think they be?
Lindsey, Myah, and Baby Girl Grace
And all of them lived with me.

2003: By the second year, Myah changed from calling me Nana to Mama. A year after that, Lindsey switched to simply Mom. Kayla's feelings were hurt tremendously. She felt as though I was shoving her out of her children's lives. However, that was not my intention. Letting them call me Mom (which did not originate from me) was to help them feel like their peers. My youngest daughter, Angela, still lived with us and called me Mom. Their friends lived with moms. They understood that I was really their grandmother but they preferred calling me Mom. I have to admit, it was comforting to me as well - I was living the life of a mother, not a grandmother.

While they called me Mom, to add insult to injury, I allowed them to call their mother "Kayla Mommy." That seemed like such a good choice at the time, but in retrospect it was a terrible idea. I wish I had insisted that they simply stick to "Mommy." There are several decisions I made over the years that I would recommend that others *not* make, but I was in emotionally-charged, uncharted territories without a road map and took detours that I now wish I had not taken. However, taking the children and raising them for those years was not a decision I ever regretted.

Grace was almost a year and a half before she could eat solid foods. She would simply gag and choke on most food. I also took her to a *"how to feed a baby" specialist.* I do not remember what her real title was and didn't even know there was such a thing. It was a full year before Grace could drink more than 3 ounces of formula at a time. That is why the feedings were so frequent. As she grew, she did outgrow many of our early health concerns and had no permanent damage from her prematurity. She was always small for her age, but she was perfect, except for asthma which she outgrew. Myah adjusted well and made friends easily. She had a bit of the dramatic flair about her, so we dubbed her our drama queen, which she didn't like. I explained that Angela was my drama queen, too, but that did not appease her. When Myah was three, she did a typical thing when she found a pair of scissors – she gave herself a haircut, a very choppy haircut at that. My daughter Katherine, who was living with us at the time, attempted to even it out by cutting it even shorter. In an attempt to make a point to Myah, Katherine told her, "You look like a boy now. I am going to call you Martin." We were not prepared for the fact that Myah would actually like that idea. When she went to daycare, the worker kept trying to get her attention. "Myah, Myah," she called. Finally she looked at her coworker and asked, "Isn't her name Myah?" Myah looked at both of them and responded, "My name is Martin." She went through a phase where she would only answer us if we called her Martin. We all found that hilarious, including Myah. I guess she got the last laugh after all.

Lindsey had a more difficult time adjusting to everything. She remembered details of her past, mostly the bad. This affected how she interacted with her peers, her concentration level, and her fears that a "bad" man was going to break into our house and kidnap her. It took years for her to quit fearing that someone was going to "steal" her. I believe what actually helped her get over that fear was an incident that occurred when she and I came home rather late one evening. Everyone had gone to bed, and we were locked out of the house. *Why I didn't have a house key on my key ring I will never know,* but I didn't. We tried all of the doors and windows and banged very loudly on the door. We could not get in and no one awoke to open the door for us. Lindsey was able to see that not just any key opened our door. Unless someone had the *right* key, they could not get into our house. I prepared for us to sleep in the car. I then looked one last time through the glove box and to my surprise found the extra house key. We slept safe and sound in our own beds that night, and Lindsey worried less from that point on about a stranger using his own key to sneak into our house.

Early on, it became apparent that the marriage I had been so hopeful about was strained, terribly strained. We did not argue, fight, or have any contention between us, at least not in the early years. There was just no emotional connection between us except for the children; caring for them was the only thing that brought meaning to our relationship. Beyond that, we were just two adults living in the same household, doing family type things with empty hearts for each other. The only things we talked about were the little ones or my grown children. My husband had two grown sons of his own but had not been very involved in raising them. Raising three little girls was completely new to him. He was more comfortable carrying our dog around the house than helping me with the children. I often heard myself complaining, "Would you please put that dog down and help me with these children." After that first long, difficult winter, we did numerous toddler and baby-friendly activities: trips to the apple orchard, walks around the neighborhood, playing in the sand at our local lake, not to mention the elaborate wooden play equipment we built for them in our backyard. Meanwhile our marriage did not flourish.

Grace in her front-pack while on Lindsey's school's field trip to an apple orchard

CHAPTER 3

There was an old woman who lived in a shoe
She had 3 darling children, yet her health became blue

2004: Even though my love for the girls grew beyond words and raising them added purpose to my life, my physical health suffered. Along with menopause, I had tremendous difficulty sleeping. I also experienced some unusual episodes similar to complex partial seizures. I called them *events*. The first one occurred while sitting in a restaurant across from my husband during one of our very few *couple-only* dates. I started feeling strange, very strange. I was dizzy and very nauseated. I stared at him but could not speak. I could see and hear him talking to me and waving his hand, "Hey, are you there? Is something wrong?" I only stared and uttered nothing. What made things feel paranormal was the *dream* I had while in this somewhat hypnotic state. I experienced a different world: I saw a church, a village with people congregating and visiting, a beautiful hillside, and the path on which I walked. As my consciousness returned to reality, I was overcome with nausea and barely made it to the restroom before vomiting in the toilet. These *events* only occurred every couple of months or so, but they were definitely frightening. What seemed even stranger was that during each *event* I had the same *dream / vision* which was much more detailed than I could remember. But when they happened, I would recognize them, *Oh yes, I saw and heard this last time.* I saw the same in-depth details that I saw before. But when I returned to normal consciousness, all I could remember was the church, the hillside, and a vagueness about the village and walking path. I feared that something was terribly wrong with my brain. I knew

I was exhausted and existing on very little sleep, but nothing made sense. I was afraid I was having some type of break-down. There was no way I was going to a doctor and risk having him tell me I was having a psychotic break and should not have the children. Finally, after having one of my *events* and throwing up and fainting in front of Angela - she cleaned up my vomit - I finally went to my doctor. I was subjected to every medical test imaginable – EEG, MRI, a brain scan, and testing for Multiplesclerosis (MS). Yet, these *events* defied them all. Neurologists had no idea what was happening to me so they called them pseudo-seizures. They explained that, while they appeared to be some type of seizure, they were not caused by epilepsy. I was also told I had a lesion on my brain, but since it was not growing it did not mean anything. I was given medication for seizures, which made everything worse by making me appear and feel stupid. I could not think clearly, my memory was scattered, my body shook, and I could not write even a simple email without having someone proofread it to ensure it made sense. I did an Internet search and found others who claimed that the medication for seizures had made them "stupid" as well. They had experienced the same reaction that I had and used the same descriptive word: *stupid*. When I called the neurologist and described my reaction to the drug, I was told to increase the dosage. Yes, the doctor actually prescribed an increase until the side-effects became so obvious even to her that she changed me to a different drug. To my recollection, these *events* seemed to decrease or perhaps even ceased after two years. However, the side-effects of the new drug were soon evident as I was angry most of the time, to the point that I was simply mean to almost everyone. The medication was changed again. The next meds made my appetite spiral out of control, to the point that I thought I might even eat our family dog (well not quite), so I just got fat.

Angela was a busy teenager during these early years with school, musical performances, and church activities. She was wonderfully helpful with the children. Once when I asked her, "What's going on? I thought you had play practice today?" She responded, "I dropped out of the musical. You're under so much pressure, Mom, and I didn't want you to have to worry about driving me back and forth to practice." I believe she was worried about my erratic health. I broke down and cried. Being the "perfect" mother to my *own baby* was not happening.

(My biggest support team – daughters) L to R:
Jennifer, Karen (me), Angela, and Melissa

CHAPTER 4

Jack Sprat could eat no fat;
His wife could eat no lean
"Oh no, no, I'm not"

2005: After having custody of the children for about three years, I had gained 60 lbs. I went from a size 6, to a size 8, to a size 10, to a size 12, and then briefly to a size 14. I weighed more at that time than I had when I was nine months pregnant with any of my eight pregnancies. My cheeks sagged, I had jowls, and I felt awful. The weight gain was a result of a combination of changes. Menopause had blasted me. Lousy eating habits were also a big problem. I had gone from eating super healthy (e.g., homemade lentil soup, fresh vegetables and fruits, and lean protein) to eating processed foods (e.g., boxed macaroni and cheese, hot dogs, and those tasty little ramen noodles). The easy to fix foods were what the children liked most, and I just wanted to get them fed quickly and as simply as possible - anything that reduced mealtime stress. I am also sure the horrid medications contributed to my weight gain. However, I was afraid the *events* would return, so I persevered a bit longer.

My turning point happened one night when I went grocery shopping with the three little girls and Angela. I'm not sure if Angela wanted to go with me as much as I needed her to. I am guessing, however, that she preferred to push a grocery cart with a child in it than to stay home and babysit. Either way, I enjoyed her company and needed her help. In the process of checking out and trying to prevent the purchase of unexpected candy bars, I noticed how the cashier looked at me.

She looked at each of the children and then at Angela. She paused, looked at me again, and then asked, "Are you going to have a boy this time?" I stood speechless with a blank stare. After I gathered my senses somewhat, I uttered, "Oh no, no, I'm not." Those were the only words that came out of my mouth. As we left, I gasped, "This is so embarrassing." To that Angela sweetly replied, "Well Mom, at least she thinks you're young enough to be pregnant." While I *could* look at it that way, I still did not *want* to look pregnant. So I committed to change my lifestyle, to eat healthier, and to start exercising.

However, just deciding to change what I ate and how I lived did not make the pounds simply melt away. Plus, I needed more than just to lose a few pounds. I was exhausted, depressed, and on too much medication. I joined a local fitness club that had daycare for Grace. I think I might have gone twice. What was wrong with me? I was terribly frustrated and embarrassed, as I prided myself on being health conscious. I knew all about healthy eating and exercise. I had a degree in health education and had even been a personal trainer and yoga instructor a few years prior. I knew all about the various aspects of wellness: physical, emotional, social, spiritual, intellectual, and environmental. All of this education and knowledge was somewhere locked in my brain but seemed useless. I didn't feel that I was doing very well at anything. I saw women who were more organized, made more money, seemed more cheerful, and just seemed to have things together. But when I thought about everything I was trying to do, I realized I didn't really think they would do any better than I was doing if they were in my place.

At some point, I said, "enough is enough." I told my family, "We are going to start eating right, and I am going off the horrible medication." I also told them to put me in the hospital if I totally flipped out on them. I was also concerned that the *events* would start happening again. I didn't really know what to expect, especially since I didn't even know what was wrong with me and neither did the doctors. While I am not recommending that others handle things the way I did, it worked for me. I stopped the neurological medication, went to a psychiatrist, focused on eating nutritious food, and tried to be more physically active. While the psychiatrist agreed that I suffered from anxiety and depression and prescribed an anti-anxiety medication (rather than the neurological medication), he assured me that I did not have an anxiety disorder, clinical depression, or any other major mental illness. Eventually, I was diagnosed with stress-induced non-epileptic seizures. I did not like the diagnosis, but it was at least something I could keep under control with awareness, prevention, and proper care.

Years later while experiencing and developing my own spiritual wellness – with the belief that spirituality is an experience and an awareness, not a belief - I came across the book, Spiritual Emergency *When Personal Transformation Becomes a Crisis*, edited by Stanislav Grof, M.D., and Christina Grof. They explain that non-ordinary experiences or a non-ordinary state of consciousness, not caused by an organic disorder that results from an identifiable mental illness, can actually result in a transpersonal spiritual experience when understood and dealt with appropriately. Whether or not my *events* could be considered organic or not, they were definitely *non-ordinary* and may actually have been beneficial had I not been so frightened of them. Years later, I am less frightened by them but still wondering how they fit with all of the other *non-ordinary* experiences I have had and continue to have in my life.

Even when those *events* ceased, I continued to struggle with fatigue and stress. However, I did lose the excess weight. My physical health improved, or at least I lost a few dress sizes. At first, I was doubtful and not sure if I should get rid of all my *fat* clothes. I had even bought two sizes of my favorite skirt, a size six and a size twelve. I guess I figured it would be less obvious that my weight was fluctuating if it looked like I wore the same skirt often. It was bizarre, but those strange *events* did not recur again for several years, and then only rarely. I can only surmise that they were caused by mismanaged stress. They also taught me to become self-aware of how I reacted to very stressful events or relationships and when to make necessary changes.

Many women and men who are doing what I was doing struggle to maintain or improve their physical health. Through my own research involving over 4,000 grandparents (91.6% women) who were raising their grandchildren, I found that 41.7% suffered with weight issues, 13.4% with diabetes, 33.4% with some form of cardiovascular disease (CVD), and a whopping 65.7% from big-time stress. Strangely though, only 9.9% of these same grandparents rated their overall health as poor. What's the deal? One-third of these grandparents were already dealing with high blood pressure and/or high cholesterol and over 13% already had diabetes (not counting those with pre-diabetes who didn't even know it), yet only 9.9% believed they had poor health. What does this tell us? It tells me that some of us do not take our own health seriously enough. We make the health of our grandchildren a high priority, which is good, while we neglect ourselves, which is not good. What will it take to make us take care of ourselves without feeling guilty? As for the guilt; we are really good at heaping it on. But to get rid of unwarranted guilt, we need to deal with our own emotional wellness.

While I consider proper nutrition to be the foundation of physical wellness, being physically active and getting enough sleep are also important. I can almost hear your moans and groans, or am I just hearing my own? Whether my problems were all caused by stress, menopause, or whatever, I could not relax enough to sleep properly. One day while in the grocery store (these trips seemed to be my main outing besides the pediatrician at that time), I picked up a magazine that caught my eye because of an article about sleep. I added it to the groceries in my cart. I would read it later when I got home. I sort of read it later. When I finally did start to read it, I discovered that it was written by a young man who had no children. He explained the importance of getting a full eight or nine hours of uninterrupted sleep each night. At that point, I tossed the magazine into the trash. It was not that I disagreed with him. It was just that his writings were so out of the realm of my reality that I just could not deal with it. While I personally had fairly good control over what I ate and whether or not I was physically active, getting adequate sleep was elusive. How was I supposed to make myself stay asleep and have happy dreams while I was constantly being awakened either by children or a snoring husband? I'm still trying to figure that one out. I knew a few tips for better sleeping such as avoiding caffeine or sugar at night, turning off all electronics a half hour before going to bed, and not getting into a heated discussion at bedtime. Some people suggest reading (something boring) before going to sleep, but that didn't work for me. Even reading a grammar book couldn't put me to sleep. What I did learn was that some things you just have to survive until they improve. Babies do eventually sleep through the night, and one way or another life does change, hopefully for the better.

I know that not all grandparents shared my experiences. While communicating with Sandy, a forty-five year old grandmother, she claimed to have none of the experiences that I had. She had not gained excess weight nor had her health tumbled. She felt her health had actually improved while raising her granddaughter. She did have a chronic health issue, but she had dealt with that for years, even as a young woman. Even though she still had children of her own at home, including one with ADHD, the stress that she experienced seemed mostly caused by the long, drawn-out custody battle. She maintained a positive attitude towards her situation by successfully turning over her concerns to her attorney and putting the outcome in God's hands.

Another example was Barbara, a sixty-five year old grandmother who had raised her grandson and was then raising her eight and nine year old great-grandchildren, both of whom suffered from ADHD and emotional trauma. Barbara's health was poor and her experiences seemed more difficult than either Sandy's or mine. Barbara didn't have money to pay for an attorney, and social workers with her local agency accused her of simply being too old to raise children, rather than providing her with emotional support and the resources she needed.

The oldest grandmother raising a grandchild that I personally knew was Edith. Edith was eighty-one when I met her. She had raised her great-grandson who was just graduating from high school. While Edith was upbeat and had a marvelous attitude about her situation, she walked slowly and painfully.

Then there was my dearest friend Betty. I loved Betty. Betty enjoyed telling me about the years she had raised her grandchildren. That was before she had a stroke and the grandchildren were sent to live with their other grandmother. Betty would tell me about her Irish grandmother, her Black grandmother, and her Native American grandfather. She had many stories to tell about her grandchildren and her grandparents. Even though Betty was much older than I, we were like spirit sisters. When I needed a break from the stress at home, I would go to Betty. I would often sit and rub her sore, swollen feet and listen to her stories that spanned three generations.

Whether we are in our 40's or all the way into our 80's, we will obviously experience different health risks. As we age, serious health conditions become more common and even fatal. It is one thing when grandpa dies of a heart attack or grandma has a stroke and grandchildren grieve from a distance. It is another when you are your grandchild's sole caregiver and you have a heart attack or stroke. This does happen. Textbooks are written and many websites are dedicated to issues concerning health and aging. I know of none that are specifically written about health and aging while raising children.

Being a healthy parent is important at any age. However as we age, many things become much more difficult. I was no exception. While I loved having my grandbabies, it took a toll on my health. It brought love and enthusiasm into my life, but it also brought health challenges. Maybe I would have experienced those difficulties anyway. That I will never know. I do know that I found it really hard to take care of myself and the children at the same time. Raising the grandchildren for those years wasn't really that much different than raising my own children, especially since I had raised children continually for over thirty years. The difference was mainly - even though I was reasonably healthy - my health at fifty-five was not what it had been at twenty-five.

CHAPTER 5

*There was a little girl who had a little curl
right in the middle of her forehead.*

Grandparents' personal concerns are not only about being physically healthy while raising grandchildren. Emotional health can also be a challenge. One difference between raising grandchildren and raising our own children is that we are not raising grandchildren for a happy reason. While we might be willing and even happy to be raising our grandchildren, someone is hurting: the parents, the children, us, or maybe all of us. One grandmother disagreed with me, "I was happy raising my grandson," she told me. That was not my point. I was willing and happy to have my grandchildren, too. I loved having a baby and small children again, but it was not for a happy reason. While my daughter called me because she needed my help, she was not happy at all. She was hurting terribly. This loving grandmother that I mentioned also had a daughter who could not care for her own son for years. My belief is firm; when we raise grandchildren or another relative's child, it is never for a happy reason. Someone is hurting.

I would like to distinguish between raising grandchildren and being a caregiver. In some agencies and programs the words are synonymous, but to me they are like night and day. The only similarity between these two types of grandparents is that they both spend a lot of time supervising grandchildren. Raising grandchildren takes caregiving to a whole new level. A grandparent who considers herself a *caregiver* probably is not the one making all of the difficult decisions, the one legally responsible for the child's total welfare, or the one who pays for everything. When I think of being a caregiver, I think of caring for an elderly parent or babysitting grandchildren while the parent works. I have been in both positions. I have been a grandparent raising grandchildren, and I have been a caregiver for grandchildren. I found being a caregiver much easier than having the sole responsibility of raising the children. As long as the parent is responsible, being a supportive caregiver can be very rewarding. However, it is still not something every grandparent is cut-out to do. Whether you are grandparent who is responsible for raising grandchildren or being their caregiver, dealing with potential conflicts is important.

The conflicts that often occur between family members can damage everyone's emotional wellness. In my case the conflicts and contentions among the adults were far more damaging to my own personal emotional welfare than conflicts with the grandchildren. As with the little girl with the curl in the middle of her forehead - who when she was good she was very, very good, but when she was bad she was horrid - our conflicts were horrid. Too much attention and energy were spent on what was not going right and what or who caused all of the problems in the first place. While I admit to having emotional issues when I raised my own children, the emotional difficulties were caused by different reasons. The first time, I was a very young, naive mother. I had my first baby at 19 and my last baby (number 8) at 33. That was by choice. I had wanted a large family and believed my marriage would last forever. I was young and optimistically hopeful. The first time around I wanted to be the model mother. I taught my kids how to read before they went to school (even home-schooled them for a few years), made homemade bread and healthy food, read and sang to them regularly, and took them to church every Sunday. I always thought I would write a book about being a "successful" mother, whatever that meant. By the time my kids reached their teens, I gave up on the silly book notion and faced my own reality. While one of my kids once said to me, "Mom, you are a good mother. You have always been a good mother to me," another one calmly told me, "I have NO good memories of growing up in our family." All I said was, "I am sorry you feel that way. I have a lot of good memories of you growing up." Having raised so many children who all had very different personalities, strengths, and weaknesses, I thought I was prepared for round two.

When it came time for a second round of raising children I was not young, but perhaps I was still naïve. When I got custody of the grandchildren, I was not prepared for the confusion, guilt, and unnecessary blame that came with it. Grandparents are well aware of the emotional trauma and problems children experience and bring with them when they lose their parents. However, we may ignore our own emotional trauma or the trauma of our own child. We may blame our children for not getting their act together. We may even blame their friends or spouse, the lousy schools, or the inadequate government agencies. Quite often we blame ourselves for the mistakes we made as parents. None of this blaming does any good. In reality, making such judgments and directing blame towards anyone does nothing but harm. It harms our grandchildren; it harms our grown children; and it harms us. It damages everyone's emotional wellness. An important lesson is that we must forgive, whether we need to forgive ourselves for our past mistakes or others for their past or present mistakes. The definition of forgiveness is to stop resenting or blaming someone for something, including ourselves. The origin of *forgive* in Old English means "to give." While you are wrapping your mind around that definition, just know there are no easy 1-2-3 steps to forgiving. One thing for sure is that when we forgive, we are the ones who have the most peace of mind. That does not mean that people do not need to change poor behaviors. It does, however, mean that if we wait until we believe that forgiveness has been *earned*, we may suffer an inordinate amount of time.

Forgiveness and healing are partners. While I wanted to help heal my granddaughters' pain, I realized that I was hurting too. I was isolated with no friends. My social wellness was practically non-existent. In the beginning, my only support system consisted of a few of my grown daughters. Angela, by then a college student, came home to visit and always cheered me up. Jennifer, a married daughter, had two small children of her own and lived an hour away. Jennifer and I were quite like sisters with children about the same age. The problem was that she didn't need another sister; she had four of them. She needed a mother. She needed a grandmother for her children. We got together as often as we could; we talked while the children played. Katherine, another daughter, lived with me for a brief time when she was expecting Ivan. She helped the best she could. However, I am sure it is safe to say that my daughters got really tired of being their mother's sole emotional support. They were certainly loving and good about it *most of the time*, but I could almost hear – and I could definitely sense - their silent groans every time I opened my mouth. They had their own lives to live and problems to solve. They didn't need mine.

Jennifer and I got away and went to a bed and breakfast inn one weekend, just the two of us. We had dinner in the dining room and talked and laughed about everything under the sun. I have no idea what was so funny, but we did a lot of laughing and had a wonderful time. The owner of the inn watched us carefully for a while and then walked over with a puzzled look and bemused smile to say, "I can't believe you two are mother and daughter. You look like best friends." Well, we were. That was good for me but not really as good for Jennifer. I believe her concerns for me just added unnecessary stress on her, and I was too overwhelmed to prevent it.

I eventually participated in a church to find emotional, social, and spiritual support and to improve wellness in each of these areas. I did find support, yet I don't believe I received the best *kind* of support. Everyone was well intended, and what I got was total affirmation that my way was the right way. It was God's way and the only logical way to see things. That perception caused major problems when I sensed Kayla wanted her children back. I wasn't about to budge and all of my church friends agreed. The children would be doomed; they would be irreparably harmed if I let them go, never to survive. The sad thing that destroyed my peace of mind and probably Kayla's, too, and so damaged both of our emotional wellness, was that I truly believed this to be true with every bit of my soul. It was up to me and only me to keep the children safe and to raise them. I was certain of that, and my support team backed me up all the way. We were definitely all sincere and truly wanted what was best for the girls, and it seemed so obvious to almost every one that my way was by far the best and only way to go. This type of thinking wreaked havoc on my own emotional wellness. It probably did not help everyone else's either. It is rather ironic that while I searched for social and spiritual support and wellness, it ended up having a negative effect on everyone's emotional health. I don't think it is supposed to work that way. Social wellness ought to help open our view to all possibilities rather than make us narrow-minded. If we are not careful, we will search out only friends who support our own point of view rather than helping us grow and be open to all that life truly has to offer and all of its possibilities.

CHAPTER 6

As I was going to St. Ives

2006: As the children grew, our outings became more elaborate and further from home. We took them to a boat show in Richmond and a Harley motorcycle show out in Louisa County. They enjoyed posing for pictures on the boats and bikes. We camped in our camper, hiked through a state forest, took them to Renaissance Fairs, and enjoyed numerous other outdoor activities together.

L to R: Myah, Grace, and Lyndsey at a Renaissance Fair

We went to parades, county festivals, church activities, local outdoor bluegrass concerts - where the girls and I danced to the merriment of the bands around our blanket - and even visited every Alpaca farm within a 100 mile radius.

Grace (3 years old) feeding an alpaca on one of our outings.

We also took the girls on a cross country trip out west to visit my parents. Although there were only five of us, simple outings could still be cumbersome with an ice chest full of food, extra clothing (in case of mishaps), books, and paper and crayons to keep them occupied in the car. We did not have the fancy flip-down DVD player in the car, but on our long trips, I put DVDs in my laptop and put it where they could all see it. I felt like the family in the nursery rhyme of St. Ives.

As I was going to St. Ives,
I met a man with seven wives,
Each wife had seven sacks,
Each sack had seven cats,
Each cat had seven kits:
Kits, cats, sacks, and wives,
How many were there going to St. Ives.

Of course in this nursery rhyme only the man was going to St. Ives, but we definitely drew attention. Most people assumed the girls were our children and we were just "older" parents. Not only did we have five family members, we also had two dogs and three cats. We did not usually take the animals with us on outings, at least not the cats. The one constant thing about our activities was that they were all planned around the children. I remember very few adult activities that we did that were just for the two of us as husband and wife. As a result, we usually drove home in silence unless we were talking about the children. The grandchildren were the only connection my husband and I had. The Harley was sold to buy a mini-van, and the house was sold so we could move further out into the country. Once we concluded that the children would be with us until they were grown, we wanted to raise them on a farm, similar to how I lived when I was a girl. At least that was the intent.

As we could afford it, the girls participated in various cultural activities such as music and dance, horseback riding, and piano lessons.

Lindsey during her horseback riding lesson

We took advantage of every low-cost activity we could find. There were also two fun outdoor activities which did not require leaving our home area. One was hiking in our neighbor's pasture and walking around the cow pies. The cows were in a different pasture, so we were safe. The other was when we put a blanket on our front lawn and studied the stars at night. We even did this in the winter, bundled up in our coats, hats, and gloves and snuggled close together, wrapped in blankets as we gazed into the heavens.

Family traditions were also important to me, so as the girls grew, I taught them all of the "family songs" that I had taught my own children. Amongst the myriad of songs I knew, we sang, "Billy Boy," "The Old Woman who Swallowed a Fly," "A Hole in the Bottom of the Sea," "There's a Hole in the Bucket," "Turn Around," "Lullaby and Goodnight," "You are My Sunshine," of course "Twinkle, Twinkle Little Star," and many more. Kids cannot argue if they are singing, so we sang lots of songs.

Along with the singing, the girls learned other family traditions, like our "um bite." I learned raising my own children that who got dessert first became a major competition. Early on, we solved this problem by requiring no eating until everyone was served. The first dessert bite was then taken together with a very dramatic "um-m-m-m-m" being verbalized in unison. This tradition stuck and continues to this day as some of my children pass the "um bite" reminder on to their children. These little girls not only enjoyed our "um bite" tradition, but started a new tradition as well. If we were having a dessert, we would light an antique oil lamp, turn the lights down very low, and pretend we lived in the "olden days" while we ate it. This tradition soon became their favorite.

Kayla would come and spend at least one weekend a month with us. It was a long drive for her, so by the time she arrived late on a Friday night she was exhausted. She then left on Sunday at noon to drive home.

Kayla with her children L to R: Lindsey, Myah, and Grace

Consequently, her only time with the girls was usually one Saturday a month when she was exhausted and needed to rest. I did not show the compassion towards her that I now wish I had. I write this because I think it is only fair to her that I admit to my unsympathetic attitude towards her. Sometimes I would take time on these Saturdays to go shopping alone so she had some alone time with her children. However, something always seemed uncomfortable to me. It was as though I could feel something transpiring that I did not welcome. I wasn't concerned that she would mistreat them. It was nothing like that. But I could feel something that I did not want to feel, something uncomfortable, something I dreaded.

CHAPTER 7

Jack be nimble, Jack be quick
Jack jumped over the candlestick.
Jack jumped high; Jack jumped low;
Jack jumped over and burned his toe.

2007: As time went by, Kayla became more involved and more important in the children's lives. While I welcomed her, there was always that nagging, horrifying feeling that I consistently pushed to the back of my mind that she may actually be in a position to take them back someday. I wanted her to have a good life and to have healthy relationships, but I did not want to lose the girls. After raising them for five years, they had become *my* children in my heart and soul. They had become my identity; they had become my life. My relationship with their mother - my daughter - became more strained than ever, and I began to feel like Jack in the nursery rhyme. I was continually tripping over hurdles, painful ones.

As for my relationship with the children, my bond with Lindsey was okay, but not as strong as it might have been. Lindsey had bonded with her mother when she was small, so she never felt the need to bond with me to the same extent. That was acceptable; it was even good, and I was glad she had bonded to her mother. Myah's bond with me was strong, but she, too, felt a natural bond with her mother. She had not forgotten the emotional bond that she had developed with her mother when she was an infant and toddler. One day while we were with friends swimming at the state park, I heard her clarify who I was to her friend,

"My mom isn't my real mom. She is actually my grandmother." I knew that was normal and even healthy for her, but for me the words stung. My connection with Grace was different. It was the bond of a mother and her own child. She had never lived with her mother. Her entire life to that point had been spent with me. In the depths of my soul, she was my baby and nothing could change those feelings. I truly believed our souls had been forever connected, a connection that would prove helpful when she was older. I was living life as a mother, not a grandmother, and I did not want that to change. This disturbed Kayla as she never intended my help to extend from months into years, even though it did.

"Myah, Myah get back here. That is dangerous. Get back here," I cried as I ran and wrapped my arms around her to keep her safe. "What are you doing? Don't ever get that far away from me again. I was scared to death when I couldn't find you." I suddenly awoke shaking and frantic. The dream had been eerily real. I knew it was one of those warning dreams that I sometimes had. I knew something was going to happen, but I did not know what. Why did I have those dreams of warning when I had no idea what I was being warned about? About a week or two later another dream came, again with the same warning. "Myah get back here," I cried. I was frantic. When I finally found her, we embarked on a long journey to unknown places, with strangers assisting us the entire way. I awoke upset and confused again, and not knowing what Myah was actually going to do. I was worried. I told my husband, "Something is going to happen that is not good. I don't know if it will be in a few days or a few weeks, but something really bad will soon happen."

Within a couple of days of my *prophetic* dream, we all learned what it was about. It was in January and Jennifer and her husband Aash and their girls, Layla and Bella, were visiting for a few days. Their family had been in India for the month of December, and Jennifer felt they needed to visit us, even though they had been invited to visit other family members. Her inspiration to be with us was a miracle indeed. Katherine's young son, Ivan, was also visiting with us over the holidays. As Jennifer, my husband, and I visited, Aash was outside playing with

Lindsey and Ivan. Myah (7), Grace (5), and Bella (5) played upstairs in a bedroom. They were being unusually quiet, but Jennifer and I enjoyed the peace and quiet as we caught up on all of the holiday news. While we visited, Bella and Grace came downstairs. Grace just stood there, motionless and speechless, while Bella tried to tell us something about Myah. I thought the girls were simply tattling and at first paid little attention to them. Everything was too quiet. You know the kind of quiet that doesn't seem quite right? Jennifer suggested, "Maybe we should see what is going on." *Yes that is a good idea*, I thought. As I ascended the large staircase I uttered, "Well, it can't be too serious. No one is screaming." How I wished I could take those words back. I entered the bedroom to find Myah hanging from a low strap around her neck that had been attached to a bed, and her legs dragging on the floor. She was grey and not moving. Months before, the girls kept jumping on Grace's antique double size bed, and it kept falling apart. So to fix this, my husband had strapped the footboard together with a Harley strap. It did not look dangerous, and how she got her neck tangled in the strap we could never figure out.

At first sight, I was the one screaming. I screamed so loud and so hard my throat hurt for days. Instantly, Jennifer and my husband were in the room with me. Jennifer ran to call 911 and screamed with panic into the phone for help. I frantically tried to loosen the strap, but I did not know how. The more I tried, the tighter it got. I just kept screaming, "Get me some scissors; Get me some scissors. They're in the kitchen." My husband, of course, knew how to use his strap so he quickly loosened it. After we released the strap and removed it from Myah's neck, we performed CPR on her. At that point, she gasped and threw up all over me, only then to inhale the vomit. This prevented her from being able to breathe. I placed her belly down on top of me on the bed. Each time I hit her back with the palms of my hands, she gasped. If she were gasping, I knew she was getting some air. Because we lived so far out in the country, it took twenty to thirty minutes for a rescue team to arrive. It felt like hours. When my arms went numb and would no longer work, I screamed for my husband to take her and keep her gasping. As soon as the feeling came back into my arms, I grabbed her back and continued. If I stopped hitting her on the back, she stopped gasping and breathing. There was no stopping until the paramedics arrived, along with the firemen, the police, and someone else that I now do not remember. Wearing a long cotton dress with a farmer's wife type apron on and covered with vomit, I climbed into the ambulance with Myah and held her hand while the paramedics continued working on her. We drove to a large parking lot where a helicopter met us so she could be airlifted to the University of Virginia Medical Center in Charlottesville, Virginia. I was not allowed to go in the helicopter and had to ride in the car. Before leaving, a paramedic insisted on taking my blood pressure as I myself was ashen, shaking, and faint. Once she determined that I was not also going to need an ambulance, she let me get into the car with instructions that I not drive.

It took us almost an hour to get to the hospital, yet when we got there the helicopter had still not arrived. I was in complete panic. I also stunk really badly, which at that time did not concern me. My husband had driven Jennifer and me to the hospital while Aash stayed at our home with the other children. We were led into a small private waiting area to wait for news. After another fifteen or twenty more minutes, we could hear the helicopter landing. No one could tell me if Myah was still alive. Soon a social worker and chaplain entered the small private room. On television, when a chaplain and social worker want to talk to the family privately, it is because of bad news. I thought I would faint at the sight of them. They assured me that Myah was still alive, but that is all they would say. Eventually, I was called back into the exam room to talk to the doctors who were working on her. They asked me if Myah often bruised herself. I told them, "All of the time. She climbs trees and monkey bars and always has bruises of some sort. In fact right now she has a very large ugly bruise between her legs that occurred when she was jumping on her bed a few days ago and straddled the headboard on her way down." I had no idea that they were quizzing me about the bruise that they had already seen. They were concerned about possible child abuse and wanted to know what I would tell them on my own. I later realized that many of the questions they asked me or things they did were to determine if we were neglectful or abusive to the children or if Myah might have intended to hurt herself. Even the complete body x-rays they took were to look for old broken bones (there were none) as part of their investigation. I am glad I was ignorant and did not realize what they were doing at the time.

Myah was eventually taken to the PICU (pediatric intensive care unit) where she remained for almost ten days. This experience was by far the most frightening and traumatic event of my life. As Myah lay in the bed, hooked to tubes with a face now swollen and covered with red spots (broken blood corpuscles), it was uncertain if she would live. If her brain started to swell, she would die quickly. With strangulation, doctors could not operate to prevent swelling since there was no local injury. It was merely a wait and see situation. I was in a hellish panic and could not think rationally. I would not leave Myah's bedside except to go to the bathroom. I would then literally run to the bathroom and run back to her room, not wanting to be gone even for thirty seconds. I lived in that vomited-on dress for two days until my husband brought me clean clothes that did not make me appear Amish. I later learned that the rescue workers wondered if I were Amish because of the way I was dressed. They didn't think so because I didn't have anything on my head. Yet everyone who did not know me was surprised when they saw me clean and in slacks.

The very first night of Myah's hospital stay I made a selfish decision. It is one I have regretted ever since, as I did not handle it kindly or gracefully. I knew I needed to call Kayla, and I needed to call her soon. It was late on a Saturday evening by this time. I so did not want to deal with the animosity between us. I talked with the doctor and he suggested I wait a few hours to call her. He must have suggested that because of the state of mind I was in, and I gladly accepted his advice to wait; however, I would never have wanted anyone to have done that to me. Still, that is what I did. I waited until about 1:00 or 2:00 a.m., thinking I would get Kayla's voice mail and she would come down the next day. No such luck. Kayla picked up the phone and I had to give her the terrible news. She and her boyfriend left immediately and arrived a few hours later. All I could think about was not leaving Myah's side. My fear, panic, and irrational thinking caused me to show no compassion toward my own daughter.

With anxiety, panic, and extreme ungracefulness, I made another poor decision. It is difficult to even write about, as I am not proud of my behavior and even the memory causes anxiety. But I believe I owe this acknowledgment to Kayla. Since there was only one cot in the room, I claimed it. I would not leave the room or even share. Kayla and her boyfriend stayed at the Ronald McDonald house free of charge at night while I slept in the room with Myah. I am not sure Kayla ever forgave me for my lack of compassion towards her. I only thought of myself and Myah. After a few days, the nurses and doctors were so sick of our contention that we were told we would be kicked out of the hospital if we didn't solve our differences. After that we took turns. I went home while Kayla slept in the room, and then I returned. That should have been our arrangement all along. It was all very confusing to the nurses. I could not seem to get them to understand that when Myah asked for "Mom," she wanted me. When she asked for "Mommy," she wanted Kayla. That totally confused everyone and I did not handle the situation with humility. Sometimes a crisis brings out the worst in people rather than the best, as in our case. However, I did learn that we were not the only ones in the PICU having family difficulties; there were others. When a child's life expectancy is uncertain or, worse yet, certain death is expected, interactions and conflicts among split family members can be horrifically sad and painful. The nursing supervisor sufficiently shamed me into cooperating by making me aware of another "troubled" family who awaited the imminent death of their child, a cancer patient. Kayla had been given the same warning that I had been given, even though we did not share that information with each other until years later.

That first night, as Myah lay on the bed unconscious (or heavily sedated, I don't know which), I tried to get the doctor to give me a prognosis. Of course, he could not. When I told him, "Myah is very smart. She is an A student", he responded, "I don't think you should count on her being an A student again. She will most likely have brain damage. How much I don't know. But children are amazing. Their brains can find new ways to learn and do things. Time will tell." When I asked him about possible surgery, he again explained why surgery was not an option. I didn't like his answer. I thought they could fix almost anything with surgery.

I put Myah's name on all of the churches' prayer rolls that I could find. The Jewish Chaplain at the hospital asked if she could add Myah's name to their world-wide prayer roll. "Most definitely," I told her. That night as I prayed over Myah, I placed my hands just slightly above her body. I had never prayed so hard in my life that God's healing power would flow through me and into Myah. If it had been possible, I would have given my very life energy to save her. As I prayed, I could feel a strong pulsating power flow through my hands, through Myah, and back through me. It was as though our souls were connected through one constant flow of energy. My eyes were closed and I thought Jennifer (who has an interest in spiritual healing) must be helping me because I really didn't believe that I could have felt that much power on my own. However, when I opened my eyes, Jennifer was across the room sleeping in a chair. It was one of the most amazing experiences I have ever had. A few hours later, Myah awoke. But she was by no means out of danger. When the doctor came in to check on her, she wanted to tell him something. It seemed very important to her. She could not speak with the tube going down her throat, so the doctor gave her a pencil and paper with his clipboard. She wrote, "I want water." The doctor was pleasantly stunned and smiled, "I think she is going to be just fine. She just has to get through the first 24 hours, and then we will continue to monitor her." Next, she developed pneumonia, which delayed her recovery. She spent over a week in the intensive care unit before being moved to a regular pediatric floor. Later, Myah told me, "Mom, I don't know if you will believe me or not, but when I was in the hospital I had a dream. Jesus came to me in my dream and touched me right here and healed me." She touched her forehead. All I could say was, "Myah, I have no doubt that Jesus healed you."

After her hospital release, she did not go to school for about a month. A school tutor came to our home three times a week. It took that long for the red dots all over her face to heal and for her sensitive emotions to be under control enough to attempt school. The first few days of her return to school, I would stay in the principal's office. Myah came to me whenever she felt a sense of panic. Eventually, she agreed that I could go home. I would be back in ten minutes if she needed me.

Myah was amazing. Her emotional recovery went smoother than we had anticipated, but she was still very sensitive to the commotion of the other children and to noise in general. This experience made it even harder for me to consider letting go of her and agreeing that she should live with her mother. The thought of losing her stirred feelings of pure panic within me. As a result, I hung on as long and as tight as I could, as if our very lives depended on it. Had I been able to foresee just a few years into the future, my life would have been much more bearable.

CHAPTER 8

Ring Around the Rosies

2008: The time did come when Kayla was in a position to raise her children. She had remarried and had dedicated herself to creating a good home environment. However, I sensed her marriage was truly no happier than mine. We both pretended we had the ideal marital relationship. We both did what we felt we had to do. It is interesting to what extent some women will go when it comes to – in Kayla's case, her children; in my case, my grandchildren. When it came to the girls, I could not simply give them back. I just could not do it; I would not, even as I faced the feared and dreaded custody battle. I never wanted the children to think that I was glad or even willing to have them leave. What followed was war. An ugly, angry battle between two women over three little girls had begun. For two years, we fought. We both had lawyers. Our entire family seemed to split apart as family members took sides. Legal fights such as this always bring pain, not only for the adults, but for the children as well. I wanted to go into court and show in a positive way why the children should stay with me. Kayla wanted to show why they should be with her. What resulted was a battle emphasizing who was the worst mother, not the best. Unfortunately, we both had plenty of ammunition to use against each other, encouraged by our lawyers. The children's attorney – a Guardian Ad Litem (the first of two) - visited me personally at my home and did a thorough home study. She walked through all of the rooms, looked in my refrigerator, and asked a number of questions, privately. There was something about her mannerisms that I simply did not like. Perhaps it was her arrogance or her air of superiority. I'm not sure. It was obvious that our home environment was clean and plentiful. We lived in a large, adequate home on six acres with everything the children needed. However, I did not want the children to stay with me simply because we had a nicer and bigger house. I thought that was a terrible reason. I wanted them to stay with me because that is where I believed they belonged.

After a year of fighting, the judge ruled in my favor. Kayla was granted visitation of two weekends a month and six weeks during the summer. Going into legal or personal details of the court proceedings here would be unproductive and even destructive to my family. Grandparents and relatives who have gone through the same thing already know the stress and harm that can be done to a family. Those of you who have not been through it should avoid it if at all possible. Irreparable damage may be done to those you love the most, not to mention the huge financial cost that may consume everything you have, even the equity in your home and possibly your entire savings. The constant planning, talking, and breathing the negative issues about the situation causes wounds to fester and consume your life. It was really hard to go through what we experienced without constantly living in a state of crisis. It affected everything and everyone. Just because I walked out of the courtroom that first go-round as the supposed winner, I did not walk out feeling good about what had transpired. I was not cheering. While I had gotten the result I wanted, the entire process had sickened me. There really was no result that would have left me feeling satisfied; too much damage had been done. In fact, more problems were yet to come as we dealt with a rigid visitation schedule and the contention and heartbreak that appeared would never end. *(Legal experiences from others are found in Part Two of this book.)*

Summer 2008 was the first time the children had ever been away from me for more than a few days. To put it mildly, it was extremely difficult. I won't explain all of the problems and gory details of visitation conflicts because, again, grandparents who have dealt with the same things already understand it too well. If you have not had to face it, I recommend you try to avoid it. We were somewhat like a dysfunctional divorced couple fighting over the children and wanting to be the "good" parent. At the end of the summer, the scheduled weekend visitations began. Living four hours apart made them difficult. We would drive and meet half way every other Friday evening to take the girls and then again on Sunday evening to pick them up. My husband usually drove with me. After leaving the children with Kayla, we fought all the way home. When we drove to pick the girls up, we argued all the way there. Yes, by this time our dysfunctional marriage had deteriorated into arguing whenever the children were not there; I do not believe we argued in front of the children, but their memories of that may be better than mine. We simply did not discuss it. I only remember a few of the things my husband and I fought about, but I vividly remember how miserable we were.

The next several months dragged on slowly. I was concerned that the tensions within the family affected the girls in school. I spoke with their teachers to check on their behavior and schoolwork. I was continually assured that they were managing very well. Neither their schoolwork nor their behavior seemed to be changing, according to the teachers. I did not discuss custody details with the children and tried to protect them from the stress that I was feeling, but it is not logical to even think I was successful in my efforts.

At night, Grace still crept quietly into my bedroom to cuddle up and sleep with me. Sometime in the middle of the night, I would hear my bedroom door slowly open and the old wooden floor creak. Little footsteps would come toward me and I would feel a tug on my arm. I would whisper, "Grace, go back to bed." Without a sound, I felt another tug on my arm. This was repeated several times. She never spoke a word, only tugged on my arm. I tried so hard to sound firm, "Grace, get back in your own bed." We knew the comfort we both felt when she climbed in bed with me. She persisted until I finally relented and instructed, "Okay, just don't wiggle and don't touch me. I need to sleep." I would pick her up and lift her over me until she settled down, almost on top of me. "Grace you can't lie so close. I can't sleep. You need to move over." She would move maybe an inch and hang on to my arm. "Grace, I can't sleep with you hanging on to me. You need to move over." Grace also knew I would eventually cave on this as well. So we settled on holding hands. I would lie there until I could feel her little body go limp as she drifted into sleep. I would then gently let go of her hand, roll over, and eventually go back to sleep. Those were almost nightly rituals, cherished memories I will never forget. Memories that would eventually be included with even more happy memories, just not yet.

CHAPTER 9

Ladybug, Ladybug fly away home.
Your house is on fire and your children are gone.

Summer 2009: Kayla just *knew* that the children should be with her and continued the battle until a different judge ruled *temporary custody* in her favor. She was elated; I was devastated and felt completely destroyed. I felt as though my heart had simply been ripped from my body. A *temporary custody* arrangement was not in anyone's best interest, especially the children's. Knowing that I simply could not agree to let the children leave, I had prayed that if that was best for the children, that God would simply make the judge rule that way. But *temporary custody?* - I knew that was not good for anyone. Since it was apparent that Kayla really was in a position to raise her own children, it did not feel moral to keep the battle going just because I wanted to keep them. Although my heart was broken, this gave me the shove I needed. I went to the children's lawyer (the second one whom I liked) and requested, through buckets of tears, that she present to the judge my decision to completely withdraw from all custody disputes. I did not request legal visitation rights with the children, either. I believed that if Kayla was to have sole custody of her children, she should decide how to raise them and I should finally bow out and let life take its natural course. Because of the animosity between us, I believed Kayla would never allow the children to even see me. My relationship with them was put on hold. I cried - heaved tormented tears - daily for months, barely functioning for almost a year. I could not fathom how my heart could feel like it was literally being squeezed to the point that I could barely breathe,

41

and yet still kept beating. My depression deepened so severely that my daughter Jennifer insisted that I come and live with her family. She was very concerned for my welfare and feared I would waste away from not eating. I stayed with Jennifer, her husband, and their two little girls for several months. My grief permeated everything around me and made it difficult to even be an engaging grandmother with her girls. This only decreased what self-esteem I had left. I am sure it did not feel good to Jennifer's family, either. It was definitely an experience none of us care to repeat.

My worst fear when letting go of the children was that Grace would forget all of the good memories we had experienced together and would simply forget me. I can see now, as I look back, that I excessively worried needlessly, but at that time I could not be consoled. Myah and Lindsey were older so I worried less about them, but Grace was not quite seven when she left and went to live with her mother. As I looked back on my childhood, I had very few memories of my life prior to the age of seven. The few memories I had of being six were not pleasant, and I had no significant memories prior to that. The only good memory I had from when I was six was the kindness of my older brother, Perry. I felt safe and protected by him. Everything else prior to six years old was simply blank or so vague it had no meaning. Because of my lack of early childhood memories, I was convinced that Grace simply would not even remember our years together. Waiting to re-establish my relationship with her until she was grown felt like a series of interminable obstacles. As mentioned, I worried less about Myah and Lindsey, not because I loved them less, but because their bond with their mother had always been stronger than their bond with me.

During this time of unrelenting grief, I sought help from various sources to no avail. I tried several traditional counseling techniques (by trained psychotherapists and religious counselors) that did not help me. I finally resorted to a non-traditional spiritual mentor. I was a bit skeptical, but I also trusted my own intuition that if she were a total flake, I would know it. How it all transpired, I cannot really say, but she was the most helpful of all. After two hours of counseling with her, I knew that the bond between Grace and me could never be broken. I also understood why it was so important and necessary that Kayla had gotten her children back, that she was the one who needed to finish raising them. This spiritual advisor felt prompted to tell me that I was supposed to help Kayla in parenting the children. She was adamant in her feelings. However, I literally laughed at that idea. "She won't even talk to me. I doubt she will ever want my help again." She believed I was wrong. She felt certain that, "The children will be back in your life in a significant way, and it will be before they are grown." I left feeling skeptical, yet clung to the idea that my bond with Grace *could not* be broken. This belief brought desperately needed relief to my grieving heart. I left with the horrible feeling of hopelessness lifted. I was not instantly healed and happy, but I was closer to something that resembled peace. As for the suggestion that I would play a significant role in the lives of Kayla and her children again, I just shelved that idea. At least I did for the next four years. One thing I did not understand or could not even comprehend at the time was how fortunate I really was that I was even dealing with this particular pain. Over the years, I have heard so many stories from grandmothers who never had to *lose* their grandchildren because they lost their own child to death instead. If I could have had the perspective of gratitude that at least my own daughter had not died, I would have suffered less.

Fall 2009: By this time my marriage had long ended. Leaving the farm and my marriage was in one sense an easy thing to do. I did not grieve the loss of my marriage, but I did tremendously grieve the loss of my home and everything it represented. I had many extraordinary and loving memories of our years on the farm, but that is also where my heart was shattered. It wasn't really a farm; it was a 110 year-old farm house on 6 ½ acres, but I called it a farm. After leaving, I had no desire to return. I did not want to see how the apple trees had grown that I planted for each of the girls, including Jennifer's girls, Layla and Bella. I did not want to see the three rose bushes I had planted beneath the kitchen window, one for each granddaughter – Lindsey, Myah, and Grace. Nor did I want to see the overgrown "way-back" where Myah and I had planned to create our serenity garden. Not only did I lose the security of having a beautiful home, but every bit of money I had put into it (including the inheritance from my father) was lost as the home became the property of the bank. The plan was that my husband would sell the house, but that is not what happened, and the house eventually was lost to foreclosure. I reminded myself daily, *It is just a house and someday I will have another.* I also felt that I had lived the nursery rhyme, *Ladybug, Ladybug fly away home. Your house is on fire and your children are gone.* Even though I had lost a house, I never really lost any children.

CHAPTER 10

Humpty Dumpty

Summer 2010: After living with Jennifer and her family for several months, I left and visited my son, Scott, in Louisiana for the summer. That was also a healing time with positive interaction between us. Scott and I probably have few beliefs in common, except that we love each other. But the fact that neither of us thought we needed to convince the other to believe our own views on anything made it a very enjoyable summer. Plus, it gave my grandson, Alex, and I a chance to get to know each other a bit better. I had been so consumed with raising Kayla's children that I gave little attention to anyone else's. This was not due to a lack of caring. It was because my psyche had just been overloaded from either parenting or from grieving.

I was like *Humpty Dumpty* - no one else could put me together again. It was obvious that I had to do it myself. I alone needed to pull things together and move forward. I convinced myself that even if I had to wait for ten years to see Kayla's children, they would eventually someday be back in my life. I still feared that they would forget their time with me, the songs we had sung, the games we played, how deeply I loved them, and that they might think I'd abandoned them. I reminded myself often that *God knew all along that I would only raise the children for a few years. I just didn't know it. It was always meant to be this way.*

At the end of the summer, I returned to Virginia and tried to resume a somewhat normal life. I came across a book titled, "When Everything Changes, Change Everything." I didn't read the book, nor did I even know who wrote it or what it was really about. However, the title alone was inspiring. Since my life had changed, I needed to change everything and start over. I chose to return to college and earn my master's degree. That forced me to focus on something besides what I felt I had lost. I had a Bachelor of Science degree in Community Health Education and wanted a master's degree in the same field. I did not find what I was looking for, so I chose to pursue a master's program in Psychology with a Specialization in Health & Wellness. For the next two years, I stayed in Virginia, worked part-time from my home computer doing what I had been doing for 15 years, and pursued my online graduate degree. It certainly did not encourage an active, productive social life, but that was not what I really needed at that time (even though I thought I did). It seemed whenever I got socially involved, I just found myself an emotional wreck all over again. In fact, while going ballroom dancing one evening, I met a woman who, after learning that I had raised grandchildren for several years, casually commented, "I bet you're glad you aren't doing that anymore." I knew I was not among friends, and it took every bit of self-composure not to burst into tears. All I could muster up was a short, truthful response, "I would rather be raising my grandchildren than being at this dance." It is a good thing I didn't want to dance with her.

Changing the focus of my life was my chance to concentrate on my other passion - healthy living from a mind, body, and spiritual perspective. I had a new life to create, no longer centered around being a mother to little children, but being a mother to grown children, a grandmother to my other grandchildren, and establishing a new career. I tried not to focus on the deep loss I felt at *losing* Kayla's children. However, I still sang to them when alone, blew the words to the wind, and prayed that through some manner I did not fully understand, our souls would stay connected. I believe it worked.

CHAPTER 11

Over the river and through the woods to Grandmother's house we go

2011: Kayla loved her children and decided they needed to keep a relationship with me. She did not want them to feel that either of us had abandoned them. After several months, and with much hesitation, she invited me to become involved in their lives once again. For quite some time, I could sense the unspoken, fearful, guarded emotions between us. Eventually, her resentment and fear softened and a tiny sprout of trust began to regrow. One day as I related to Kayla how I'd been thinking I might have to wait until the girls were grown to reestablish my relationship with them, she responded, "Gee, Mom. You sure don't give me much credit." I was actually relieved by her response. After two years, we were making the adjustment for me to again be the grandmother. I was now Nana again, as I was with my other grandchildren. When events first turned for the better, I would travel from Richmond, Virginia, to Maryland and stay a few days being Nana. Mending the hurts and anger that engulfed us required effort from my daughter and me. Our desire to put our family back together and help the children heal motivated us to work together, put past hurts behind us, and move forward. It wasn't easy; in fact, it was a very fragile process that took years to accomplish. Was it something that could ever be truly *accomplished*? Mending the hurt was a process that forever evolved. The road to rebuilding trust was rocky, with cliffs and valleys to say the least. My visits with the children were cherished by the children as well as myself. Sometimes I brought crystal beads to make bracelets and necklaces, ingredients to make something tasty, a new game to play, or new dance steps to teach. The first words the girls usually said with great excitement were, "Polly! Polly is here!" Polly was my pug. I was often greeted with "Did you bring your crystal beads?" or "Do we get to make fudge?" or even "Will you sing our songs to us?" On one visit, I surprised them at the bus stop. Grace smiled and said, "Mommy told me there would be a surprise after school that I would like. I knew it was you." While I became Nana again, it was obvious the special bond we had built was still there. We sang songs together and recorded them and would end up laughing so hard at our mess-ups that we couldn't see straight. Other times we curled up and rocked in the large over-stuffed rocking chair. One evening while we were shopping, I slipped up and said, "This is just like old times." I quickly added, "But these are new times." Myah replied, "New times are better than just memories." Our good memories were invaluable, but yes, the new times were definitely better than memories.

Sometimes between planned visits, Kayla would text me when someone was ill—"Can you possibly come up here and help us?" At that time, most of my work and school were all done online so my Mom Motto was: *Have laptop, cell phone, and dog - will travel.* I usually texted back that I would be there in a few hours. Even with the progress we were making, I always felt as though I was walking on thin ice, just waiting for everything to collapse. I suspect Kayla's feelings were similar.

CHAPTER 12

Hickory Dickory Dock

Spring 2012: In early 2012 due to another misunderstanding, we again went over one of our cliffs. As a result, we went through 2012 with no contact, not even phone calls or emails. It appeared we were back to square one, and I felt the raw pain as though it had never gone away.

Hickory dickory dock.
The mouse ran up the clock.
The clock struck one.
The mouse ran down.
Hickory dickory dock.

The ups and downs, the misunderstandings, and hurt feelings were totally insane. No doubt, Kayla must have felt the same way as she was the one to initiate the *stay out of our lives,* which I did. And even though I respected her request and stayed out of their lives, they were never out of mine.

As I focused on other aspects of my life, such as school and work, I had constant reminders of my life with the children. I would have frequent nighttime dreams about the girls and Kayla. Depending on the dream, I could tell when they were experiencing difficulties that were either related to or not related to me. I was very familiar with having dreams that would let me know when loved ones were experiencing trials and difficulties. These types of dreams started when I was sixteen. I don't ask for them; they just come unexpectedly. They can bring me

49

peace or can be very disturbing. If I had an unsettling dream about any of my children, I usually called them to find out what was up or if anything was wrong. I even had some of my kids say to me, "If you have a dream about me, Mom, let me know," just in case I had a helpful warning for them. However, with Kayla I couldn't just call and ask, *What's going on?*

Life got strange. My experiences were going beyond nighttime dreaming. I even had a profound non-ordinary experience during the day that was not a dream. On one of Grace's previous visits the year before, I had bought her a pair of little black shoes so she could go ballroom dancing with me. On her last visit she asked if she could leave the shoes at my house so she didn't have to carry them back and forth. "Sure, no problem. Just put them in the closet," I told her. I did not know which closet or even which room she had put them in. She knew where they were, and that is all that mattered.

Months after Grace had put her shoes away *somewhere*, I had a most unusual experience for which I still have no certain explanation. One morning I awoke to find the little black shoes sitting on the edge of my bed in plain sight. I paused and just stared at them. How did her shoes get on my bed? No one lived there but me, and I didn't even know where they had been. My first thought was one of horror. Had something happened to Grace, and did she put them there? *No, no. If something had happened to Grace, someone would have called me,* I assured myself. I could make no sense of the situation, but I felt as though I was being sent a message from someone or some entity I could not see. That thought did not frighten me, not at all. I just wanted to understand the message. So I thought about the symbolism of shoes. Shoes are used to protect one's feet. They are worn when going somewhere, like a journey. Okay, I got it - Grace was on a journey of some type. I still had no idea what type of journey she could be on.

Sometimes I thought it would have been easier to remain totally in the dark about what was happening rather than to be given smidgens of information from odd sources without the privilege of knowing the entire situation. But that's not how it happened. During that time, I had no choice but to be patient and wait for a clear picture to present itself, which it eventually did. In the meantime, I periodically had dreams that somehow mentally kept me in the loop. One time I dreamt of both Myah and Grace being with me as I was being counseled by a heavenly being named Helen. That was a most amazing dream (of course I did not remember most of Helen's advice). I also welcomed the dreams that showed me how strong Kayla was and how well she was holding up under her stressful life. Dreams such as those were always welcomed for they were reassuring and calming. There were many others that were disturbing and nightmarish that awoke me, crying and shaking. I could not tell if they were merely coming from my own subconscious mind or if there was a real message hidden in them somewhere. Then there was the dream that focused on Grace's eyes. Something in her eyes showed her detaching from something. Was she detaching from me or something else? I rarely dreamed of Lindsey. It was as though there was a block put up to keep me out. I felt as though whatever was happening in her life, I apparently was not meant to know. And so the dreams just popped up, uninvited and for no obvious reason. As I waited to find out if there were any real meaning to them, I kept them recorded in a dream journal. Later, I compared the timing of the dreams to what was really happening in Kayla's life. The dreams were amazingly well timed.

Summer 2012: For various reasons I decided to leave Virginia. I was having a difficult time finding work that was related to my education. I was also tempted to drive to Maryland just to watch the girls get off the bus. To avoid being arrested for stalking, I decided I needed a change of scenery. I needed to be somewhere that did not constantly remind me of everything I felt I had lost. However, there was a large obstacle - I had no idea where I should go. I was tempted to just pack my car and start driving and see where I landed, perhaps in some small mountain town somewhere. I simply had no good ideas. My sister Jayne did not like the idea of me just getting in my car and driving to who knows where. She suggested I come and stay with her in Florida until I figured out where I belonged. With all of the nerve and emotional strength I could muster, I gave away many of my belongings, put the rest in storage, and - with

Jayne's help - packed my car and drove to Florida, leaving just in time to miss a thunderstorm that caused a city-wide power outage during a record high temperature of 106 degrees.

After arriving safely in Florida, I still didn't know what to do. I knew no one there besides Jayne and her children. They were all wonderful to me. However, feeling like an emotionally wrecked sister and aunt was not very empowering. During this time, my mother had a stroke. My sister and I decided to bring her from Utah to Florida to take care of her. I would be the main caregiver, as we felt that was something I could do well. Once again, things did not turn out quite as expected. Mother's stay in Florida did not last long before she wanted to return to Utah where she had lived for many years. Salt Lake City had become her home and that is where she wanted to be. After Mother went back to Utah, I still could not find work that utilized my expensive education in the area where my sister lived so I decided to move to a more populated part of Florida where I was told I would have better luck.

Luck - what an interesting concept. I believe in hard work; I believe in intuition and spiritual guidance. I do not generally believe in luck. Due to my financial situation, I needed to move in with a roommate, another professional female. That seemed like a really good option while I looked for employment, and the roommate situation worked out fine for the most part. Unfortunately, I could only find part-time employment that was not only completely unrelated to my graduate degree, it actually required no education beyond high school. I soon realized that I had taken a terrible, horrible, no good, very bad part-time job and that I was unhappy with my circumstances.

Within a very short time, I discovered just how bad a job it really was. It happened during one of my shifts. While I sat in a chair working on paperwork, a coworker walked behind me without touching me. I felt a strong pressure that forced my shoulders down, preventing me from getting out of my chair. I had never felt such a physical, oppressive, negative energy that strongly before, ever. After that first experience, every time I went to work it felt as though this oppressive energy was actually seeping out of the walls. If it had been a historical war building or something related to fighting, I would have suspected that some weird paranormal activity was going on. Instead, I was told that the facility had been a boys group home before the current agency had purchased it. That still might account for it, if you believe that negative energy, evil, or sorrow can get stuck in a building. I had never believed that before, but by then I wasn't so sure of anything. Whatever it was that I had felt, it was real, and I didn't like it.

I knew my life needed to change; it simply had to change. I had worked too hard and was living on pure faith that things had to get better. And so, while 2012 felt like a year of waiting and holding, the year 2013 brought a full cycle of change, both physically and emotionally. It was the year when healing began.

CHAPTER 13

God's Gift to Me

God's gift to me is you,
But for how long I do not know.
If his gift is for eternity,
I will love you forever.
If it is for a lifetime,
I will love you till I die.
If his gift is but for a fleeting moment,
I will love you with all my heart today.
But for now dear children,
While you have captured my heart forever
And I am only a phone call away,
I must love you from the edges.

Spring 2013: 2012 came and went with no contact with Kayla or the girls. I had a hard time *getting a life*. Whatever *getting a life* meant, I was really bad at it. When I discovered just how bad my terrible, horrible, no good, very bad part-time job was, I could not even describe my disappointment. I guess I didn't do well with the huge invisible message in the building that stood for *No Creativity Allowed*. Perhaps it was better than no job at all, but I doubted it.

As I tried to *get a life*, I met a few people; I went on a blind date (with a so-not interesting man) and throughout the date could only think about how I was missing Grace's birthday. So, while I found my date very unattractive, I'm sure that he found me terribly annoying. He later emailed me and told me that maybe we should take a couple of weeks - until I was over Grace - before we met again. I literally laughed out loud; *Two weeks? Get over Grace? I hadn't gotten over the girls in over two years!* While I was very aware of why he was annoyed with me, I was also irritated at his conceit. I tersely replied to his email - "You think I will be over Grace in two weeks? If I can ever find a man who can create anything near the passion inside of me that these children do, then I will be willing to date. Until then, I will quit looking." I know my email was not polite; in fact it was quite rude. But I really thought this man was overly confident in his own personal appeal.

Nothing I was doing felt right. Nothing felt remotely like a personal mission, except the volunteering I did for a group of grandparents who were raising their grandchildren. To help grandparents, I developed a health and wellness assessment and goal setting program (*See Appendix at the end of the book*). The purpose of the program was to bring awareness to their own wellness or lack thereof and to help them set goals and discover ways to accomplish those goals. One grandmother's goal was to get her GED, which related to her intellectual wellness. Another grandmother was working on her emotional wellness by not letting others control her. One grandfather's goal was to work on his physical wellness. He joined Silver Sneakers, an exercise program paid for through Medicare. There were grandmothers, grandfathers, great-grandmothers, and other family members who participated in this program.

Volunteering with these grandparents and using my education was very important and worthwhile to me. If creating this project was the only thing that I accomplished during my year in Florida, then I had succeeded at something that was valuable to me. I received no recognition or payment of any sort from the agency that sponsored this grandparent group. I guess it was my unintentional way of *paying it forward*. For later on, I myself received much assistance from others when I was injured and had no insurance. Other than when helping with the grandparent group, I felt oddly out of place everywhere I went, except when I was with my sister, of course.

Occasionally I went out dancing with my roommate and her girlfriends. A few times I even ventured out solo, until I broke my elbow and fractured my pelvis. I had decided to go ballroom dancing on a Wednesday evening to get my mind off my less than desirable life, especially my terrible, horrible, no good, very bad part-time job. As is common in ballroom dancing, I danced with men I did not know. That evening ended when I was dropped while being dipped at the end of a waltz. To make matters worse, the man lost his balance and fell on me. The result was a fractured pelvis and a broken elbow that required surgery. The elbow - severely dislocated and broken in two places - was wired together in hopes that it would eventually heal.

After spending eight days in the hospital, I was sent home with the help of a home health aide (Valentine's Day, 2013) until my daughter, Melissa, flew in from Oregon to take care of me for a month. It was definitely a humbling experience for me, as I had never had one of my daughters have to shower and dress me. I don't know what I would have done had she not been able to come and care for me. My ability to be employed even part-time ended. My work was now limited to what I could do one-handed with my computer, such as writing for people or other such computer work. Back to my sister's I went, now handicapped. I was utterly bewildered. Could life get any worse? Of course it could, but it didn't.

About this time, I got an email from Kayla informing me that she had ended her second marriage and was returning to Houston where the children's father was incarcerated. I sensed in her email a need to explain her decision to me, perhaps hoping for my approval or encouragement. I wasn't quite sure. While I appreciated that she informed me of this most important decision to relocate, I had long believed that Kayla was being spiritually guided in her life, and I knew she did not need my advice, my opinions, or my criticism. She asked for none, so I offered none. I did, however, let her know that I trusted her.

Over the next few months, communication between Kayla and me inched forward. We started with minimal contact through Facebook as *friends* and progressed to me talking with the girls on the phone. These conversations were simple exchanges of information, *How is school?* "Fine." *What is your favorite subject?* "Math." *What do you want for your birthday?* "I don't know." *What do you like about Texas?* To the Texas question, Grace responded, "I like that there are flowers year round here." Myah's answers weren't any more detailed. It was almost as though I was a complete stranger asking some very boring, worn-out questions. Lindsey, at 15 however, had much more to say. She gave detailed monologues about school, boys, and goals for college.

Communicating with the girls gave me hope that we could rebuild our connections, but the lack of substance in most of our conversations gave cause for concern. Still, I was willing to take what crumbs I was given and create the best feast I could with them. While I didn't know what to expect - or if I should expect anything at all - I attempted to handle the situation as optimistically and gracefully as I could.

Summer 2013: Summer brought great joys and deep sorrows. I went on a trip to Salt Lake City with my sister Jayne to see our mother on her 90th birthday. We did not know it would be her last. We also visited Riggins, Idaho for several days and absorbed the fresh, energizing mountain air while hiking, sight-seeing, and visiting with my brother Perry and his wife Jeri. Ever since I was a child, I have always had a strong connection to nature, especially trees. Whether hiking in the mountains or a forest, wandering through a grove of trees, or simply touching a tree, I could find solace. Late one night, while still in Idaho, I typed slowly with mostly my one good hand. Jayne asked, "What are you doing?" I breathed a sigh of relief and simply replied, "I am writing." I could hardly believe it. I was feeling peaceful; I was able to start writing again. I accepted the fact that while I was no longer at the center of the girls' lives, I was learning to love them *from the edges*. Loving Kayla and her girls *from the edges*, however, soon took on new meaning.

It had been almost two years since I had seen Kayla and her girls. I really wanted to visit them. One evening, while battling my fear of rejection, I emailed Kayla and asked her if I could visit them for the Christmas holidays. I could get an inexpensive plane ticket by purchasing it so early, flying directly from Orlando to Houston. When she replied that I was welcome to visit, I was relieved, excited, and a bit nervous. We were moving in the right direction. Christmas 2012 had been skipped; I dodged it; I went completely around it. Other than sending gifts to my other children and grandchildren, I literally avoided it. On Christmas Day, I went to the movies with a friend. I didn't do anything at all that could remind me that it was Christmas. It had been my first year without any of my children or grandchildren, and I had successfully made it very un-Christmassy. While I avoided Christmas so as to not feel any loss, I also decided that I did not want to repeat that the next year. I intended to make Christmas 2013 a happier time, so I purchased my plane ticket immediately upon Kayla's approval.

Less than two months after spending my mother's 90th birthday with her and while still relishing the memory of the energizing Idaho Mountains, I received a message that my mother had suffered a massive stroke and would not live much longer. I made arrangements and flew to Salt Lake City in hopes of talking with her before she passed. She was placed in hospice care the day I arrived, but she never regained consciousness. Her birthday celebration two months earlier would have to suffice for my last happy memories with her. While this was not necessarily a sad situation, as she had long since decided she was ready to go to heaven, there was still something haunting me. Perhaps the melancholy feeling came from unresolved issues between my mother and me, things I wished I could have discussed with her but couldn't. Or perhaps it came from feeling her lack of approval because I had chosen a different spiritual path than hers. I never doubted my mother's love for any of her children, but in some elusive way I felt she loved me *because* she didn't really know me. These ambiguous feelings plagued me during her dying process as I realized how much daughters still need the approval of their mothers, even when they are mothers or even grandmothers themselves. My thoughts automatically went to my own children, and I knew I still had a mission to accomplish as a mother to my grown children. I didn't have a clear picture of what I was to do, just a sense of knowing that wounds still existed, and they could heal more easily with my help than without it. During the process of my mother dying, I created a Facebook message group that included all of my children. I kept everyone updated at the same time. However, the evening Mother passed, I mostly communicated with Kayla. I let her take the responsibility of contacting her siblings. Somehow it seemed appropriate and fitting, with her being my oldest daughter, that I should turn to her first. My son Briton, who lived in Utah, had been chosen by my mother to follow her wishes in regards to funeral arrangements. I stayed with Briton, his wife Amber, and my one-year-old grandson Coulsen until I flew home after the funeral. That gave me ample opportunity to focus on my feelings about mothers and their children. I even sent a mass private Facebook message to all eight of my children - *My mother wasn't perfect, but she was MY MOTHER! The only one I had, and I am your mother, the only one you have. So just remember children that someday sooner or later, I will be the one that will be in my mother's place that is naturally part of this existence. Wounds that need to heal need to heal while I am still here to help them heal. I feel a sense of urgency on this matter.*

Most of my children responded to my family Facebook message. From Angela, "I'm here for you Mama! You know that!" (Then I received a long very sweet private message from her). From Melissa, "I'm praying for your strength, Mom. I dread the day when I have to experience what you're going through." From Kayla, "I can only imagine what kinds of emotions you are being bombarded with… I'm praying for you too." From Katherine, "I love you Mom! You are in my prayers too, just like grandma." From Jennifer, "♥ ♥ ♥." From Seth, "Have a safe trip."

After the funeral, I returned to Florida with a great heaviness in my heart, feeling the need to help heal hidden wounds. If I felt that my mother loved me because she didn't really know me, perhaps some of my children felt the same way. I wanted to be certain that my children knew they were loved for who they really were, not in spite of it.

Fall 2013: As summer turned into fall, I still hoped my injury would heal and allow me to obtain gainful employment. I earned some part-time income, doing a little of this and a little of that. What I really hoped for was a position that utilized my thinking abilities without needing two good hands. I did not find anything like that. I couldn't even push a grocery cart as it required the use of both arms. When shopping, I resorted to pulling the cart with my right hand and loading groceries in and out of the car using only my good arm. It was discouraging to discover how many activities required the use of two good arms and hands. Using the computer for any extended use of time was painful, driving a car hurt, wrapping a package hurt, and even holding a book while turning pages was painful. I didn't know how to find gainful employment while thinking, *Hey, do you want to hire me? I have one good hand, and when I am not exhausted from the chronic pain, I can usually think clearly. Oh, and by the way, I am in a good mood when I am on pain pills.* No, I didn't think that would work. I was really looking for part-time work as a health coach in a worksite wellness program or a program specifically for seniors, fifty plus. I wasn't looking to be a personal trainer again or to be any type of fitness instructor. Wellness Coaching would use my training without over-stressing my left elbow and hand. Every day I tried to do something towards finding appropriate work. Between Internet searches, filling in online job applications, and refining my resume, I kept looking, but nothing came forth. In the meantime I worked a few hours here and there doing independent projects, making a very small amount of money.

I was restless living in Florida. In spite of having a bonding experience with my sister, I did not feel like I belonged there. I prayed for definite direction. *I will do whatever I am supposed to do. I just need to know clearly what it is.* I continued with my personal spiritual practice, feeling that not only did I need to find a way to support myself with an injury, but I also had been called to help heal a generation within my family. That was a lofty calling (and rather scary), and one that I had no idea what it really meant or what it entailed. It was merely an intuitive impression of an unfulfilled agreement I had made. Fortunately, the impressionistic calling was soon made *blatantly* clear.

I knew I was on a spiritual journey. I had known that since childhood. But it wasn't until recently that I actually understood that true spirituality was, in fact, a *spiritual experience,* not just a way of thinking. For example, a musician does more than just think about and listen to music. He practices regularly in hopes of creating an inspirational masterpiece. He experiences his music. The same goes for any artist. Just dreaming, imagining, and longing does not create a great piece of art. An artist does all of these things, but he also practices and lives the life of an artist. My spiritual practice was meant to create a meaningful experience, both in spirit and form. While I mentally and emotionally analyzed the different experiences in my life, I had to decide if they were benefitting or obstructing my spiritual practice, which would eventually open up my full understanding of my purpose in life. I realized everything had a purpose, even my accident and my previous part-time job. Those experiences forced me to change the direction I was headed and prepared me for something better.

In the middle of September, I received a Facebook message from Kayla wanting to know if I had found a job yet. She was very apprehensive about sharing her ongoing struggles with me as she felt that our relationship usually went from good to bad very quickly, but she didn't know what else to do or who to ask for help. After several online messages back and forth, we eventually talked on the phone. I knew immediately upon reading her first message that I was supposed to move to Houston and help her with the children. That was my *blatantly* clear assignment. I would just have to find work as a health coach in Houston, which proved to be easier than in Florida.

Even though Kayla and I both admitted to each other that we were nervous about this arrangement, it was the right thing to do. Nothing ever felt more right. I assured her I would follow her lead when it came to the children. I think her greatest fear was that I would come into her home and tell her how to raise her children. That was the last thing I wanted to do. Not only was I impressed with what a good mother she was, but my main purpose was to support her, not to rescue the children. With all of the crazy things that happen in the life of a single parent, a second parent (albeit a grandparent) was needed to help supervise, transport, and encourage children.

Within just a few days of making the decision to move to Houston and live *temporarily* (whatever that meant) with Kayla and the girls, I packed up my small car, topped with a vinyl car top carrier, and headed to Texas. I felt like the Beverly Hillbillies starting a new life. There had always been something exciting about a road trip, but that trip brought a mixture of excitement, apprehension, and downright trepidation. Still, I knew I was called on a mission - very important mission. I also knew that loving Kayla and the children *from the edges* did not mean from a distance anymore. While I was going to be literally living right smack in the middle of their lives *again*, I could only help them with problems if I did not become part of the problem or, worse yet, become *the* problem. By loving them *from the edges* of any problems and challenges, I could actually offer loving support and strength. It seemed rather like having a loved one sick in bed with a contagious illness. You can't really help them if you simply crawl in bed with them and get sick, too. No, it is better to be near and help when you can. I realized *I Love You from the Edges* applied to my other children and grandchildren as well. In fact, the concept also applies to friends and neighbors. This was a valuable lesson to learn.

I finally arrived in Houston, exhausted, without make-up, with messy hair, wearing wrinkled, baggy clothes. I had come to assist Kayla, but looking tired and bedraggled with an injured arm and aching joints, I was the one needing assistance. I had no doubt that I needed Kayla and the girls as much as they needed me.

It didn't take long to learn how I had historically been perceived in regards to Grace. According to everyone (other than Grace and me, of course), I favored her, and she manipulated me to no end. Now, while Grace and I did not see it that way, I definitely had to be careful, because *yes*, I was susceptible to her wiles.

It was an adjustment for everyone during those first couple of months. For four years, I had lived alone or with adults who did not need my attention. I had gotten used to being alone to hibernate, meditate, read, or watch TV. Apparently, Kayla was not used to seeing me spend so much time alone and didn't know if there was an issue or not. At one point, she knocked on my bedroom door. "Are you hiding from me?" she asked. She wasn't sure how to take my withdrawal. I thought that was really funny and laughed, "Of course, I'm not hiding from you. I am just reading." Nothing was wrong, absolutely nothing. When I wasn't interacting with the girls, fixing dinner, or running errands, I was working on my computer, reading a book, writing a blog post, working on a project of some sort, or writing this book, all of which I usually did in my bedroom. I thought it interesting that, while kids sometimes hide from their parents, it now looked like I was hiding from them. Perhaps I *was* hiding from everyone a wee bit, but not for any negative reasons. I was simply being quiet and being alone when not taking care of the children. Plus, I didn't like the fact that Kayla seemed to feel that she had to go outside to have a private phone conversation. She needed to maintain her sense of privacy as well.

At first, I questioned myself as to what chores I should just take on as my responsibility. Kayla had been under so much stress that I didn't want her to misperceive my intentions. It was obvious that I was the designated driver for the girls since Kayla worked full-time and I did not. Myah was on crutches due to a sprained ankle and needed to be driven everywhere, Lindsey needed to be picked up daily from school, and Grace had her occasional after-school activities. I was very glad I was there. I could not think of a sane way a single working parent could do everything that needed to be done with two teenagers and a preteen and still keep a job. We have all read about kids who got into trouble and people asked in a derogatory way, "Where were the parents?" Well maybe the parent was working, trying to keep the rent paid, and the kids were on their own too much because there was no grandparent or family member available to help. Everyone has heard the saying, "It takes a village to raise a child." Since we didn't have a village, a mother and a grandmother had to do.

Beyond being the kid transporter, I wanted to be helpful, but not intrusive. I began with simply fixing dinner. Those first few days when Kayla came home from work to find dinner on the table, she let out a huge sigh of relief, "I could get used to this." Next, I came up with a reward system that encouraged the girls to keep their rooms tidy. I was amazed at what they would do in order to have money in their pockets. I also realized how incentives needed to be flexible, as they tended to wax and wane. The girls were always going to save *their* money until they could buy something super cool and expensive. However, every time we went to a thrift store or dollar store, they always found things they *really needed*. I perfectly understood their feelings. I never liked going shopping just to look. I found it depressing to look at so many desirable things that I wanted but could not afford. If I were looking for just ideas, so I could make something creatively and cheaper or found a super deal at a consignment store, I didn't mind the shopping so much. While we creatively shopped, I found the girls very easy to please, as was their mother.

I learned so much while living with Kayla and the girls. First, I learned from Kayla's style of parenting. She thought it humorous that I believed she was stricter than I had been when she was growing up. She laughed at that notion. Was she stricter than I had been? I guess that was debatable, but she definitely had an innate ability to be consistent with the house rules she established. When my children were growing up, I would set rules or discipline someone, only to forget who I had told what. I guess that is one down-side of having such a large family. With so many children, it was easy for the wrong one to take the blame for who left the wet towels on the floor, ate the last of the pudding, or stuck gum under the chair.

Years later, my own kids still reminded me that they were blamed for things they did not do. When Myah expressed her frustration that she had been blamed for something Grace did (years ago when they lived with me), I assured her that she was not alone in her plight. My daughter, Melissa, told me how frustrated she was as a teenager when she was blamed for things Katherine had done. I, too, can tell stories about how my sister, Jayne, got blamed for something I did when we were kids. Apparently, this was a multi-generational thing. I assume my family was not that much different than other large families, despite what the children think.

A second thing I learned while living with Kayla and the girls was how nice it was being the caregiver for grandchildren rather than the grandmother who was raising the grandchildren. Even though I was mostly doing the same activities, I did not shoulder the same emotional responsibility. I was more than happy to say, *Let's ask your mother when she gets home,* or *If your mother wants it done differently, she will change it when she gets home.* I was perfectly satisfied with being Nana and letting Kayla be Mom. I also believed it would not take her long to learn that there was no threat of me usurping her authority.

Often grandmothers have expressed the frustration of not being appreciated, with never a "thank you" being spoken. I know what that feels like. When I felt that way, I reminded myself that I was not doing what I was doing to be thanked. One day, unexpectedly, I received a message from Kayla, "I appreciate your help. I don't say it enough. I'm sorry for that. You being here is making a huge difference in the girls and my lives, and that is something that will be carried on for a very long time…longer than both of our lives. It truly is a wonderful help. We love you." What a lovely message that touched me deeply. What a difference from my earlier fears that she would never let me be part of her family's life, ever again.

The third lesson that I learned while living with Kayla and the girls was how important it was for the children to reconnect with their father. I had not expected that simple, weekly letters and phone calls could be so healing for the family. Through this experience, I learned how sometimes having a daddy in prison might be better than having no daddy at all. I might not have believed in the importance of their communication had I not witnessed it first-hand. However, I recognize that this may not be the best solution for all children and in all situations. But it has caused me to pause and think about the effects on the children when I hear about someone being incarcerated. No longer do I merely think, *He probably deserved it.* My heart goes out to their children, regardless of the parents' guilt.

It was also not only different, but quite comical living with the girls as teenagers rather than as small children. I noticed when we were in public that the girls didn't like me putting my arm around them or even touching them. Of course, they acted the same way with their mother. Kayla just laughed at how funny it was that the girls were so embarrassed to be seen with her. When that first happened to me I thought, *What the heck? Even my own kids hadn't acted like that.* I did notice their behavior depended on what we were doing. If we were on *their* turf – a church youth activity or at their school – they walked about five feet ahead of me. If they were on *my* turf - a crystal and rock shop or something of the sort - they stayed close to me. Perhaps they just wanted me to buy them something. Grace tended to hang closer to me when at home than either Lindsey or Myah did. She often sat on my bed next to me, using my second laptop, doing homework while I worked on my computer. Myah and Lindsey simply asked to borrow the computer and then took it to a different room. My one-on-one time with Lindsey was usually when I picked her up from school or took her to appointments. Myah was eager to run errands and go shopping with me, while Grace preferred to stay home. It all seemed to balance out quite well.

Then there was the question of whether or not they should ask me for advice. One evening Grace (11) told me that her best friend's ex-boyfriend had just asked her to *go out* with him. I had finally learned that when preteens say they are *going out* they aren't really going anywhere. Grace asked me how she should tell him that she wasn't interested, since he was her girlfriend's *ex*. I first asked her if she liked him. "No, absolutely not," she exclaimed. "Well, I don't really know what you should say," I answered. Grace laughed and said, "When I asked Myah, she told me to you ask you, but then I reminded her that the last time she had asked you for advice about a boy, you had told her to tell him to 'jump in a lake.'" To that I replied, "Well, he must have been being rude." Myah piped up, "No, he was just telling me that I should wear my dark blue eyeliner." I remembered the conversation and told her, "Well, if a man told me I should wear more makeup, yes, I would tell him to 'jump in a lake.'" Myah asked, "Would you really say that?" To that I simply responded, "Probably not," and we laughed.

I learned with Lindsey to just listen and offer little advice. In the beginning, she might say something like, "I really made so-and-so feel badly today by something I said." I would respond with, "Well, maybe you need to apologize." Then I learned that Lindsey often over-blamed herself for everything, even when nothing was her fault. For a teenage girl who tended to hold herself accountable for everyone else's feelings, that was lousy advice. If it seemed important, I would pass the information on to Kayla – if Lindsey had not already done so – because Kayla was very good at helping Lindsey deal with her emotions.

I knew being in Houston helping Kayla was the necessary thing to do; it was what I wanted to do. But I also knew I was missing out by being so far away from my other grandchildren. While I loved the chance to go to the musical concerts at school - Lindsey and Myah sang and Grace played the violin - I missed Jennifer's and Katherine's children in Virginia and all of their performances. Plus, there was Alex in Louisiana and Coulsen in Utah. Angela, who was only fifteen when this story began (a decade ago), was now married and expecting their first child. Also, Seth had grown step-sons whom I had never even met. So this was a bittersweet situation. On top of that, I still needed to *get a life*, other than grandchildren. Grace was eleven. It would only be a few years before Kayla had no children at home. Unless I intended on continually moving around the country as my other children had babies (actually, I liked that idea), I needed a major paradigm shift in my thinking to discover what lay beyond children, grandchildren, and future great-grandchildren.

It was sometimes a terrorizing thought for me as I continued toward retirement age with no real retirement income to support myself. Consequently, I hoped that I would find other things about Texas that would make me feel like I belonged there, as I had never expected to live in Texas. It simply had never been on my mental radar. Other than the fact that I had never liked the Dallas Cowboys football team and I thought Texas *very flat*, I really didn't have much of an opinion about Texas.

That began to change. Within a short time, I found Houston an easier place to find work as a health coach. I also discovered that national and state forests, where I could enjoy trees, were only an hour away; I needed those trees. The rest I figured would come in due time. So while I saw that I still had a challenging puzzle to put together, at least I had the pieces. My vision of this most complex puzzle (my family) that I have been working on for decades and the one that has taught me to *love from the edges*, is beautiful.

CONCLUSION

A Soft Reply

I often ponder on the experiences I had and the lessons I learned. My hope is to be of help to other grandparents and relatives who experience many of the same things I did. I also hope others will learn from the choices I made, be they good or *not so good*. Grandparents and relatives raising someone else's child do so for various reasons, but one common thread is that no one is doing this for a *happy* reason. No matter how much we love these children, someone is hurting. Stepping in and being responsible for someone else's child is not always an easy decision. While it is often quite challenging, it is also most rewarding. Many grandparents find that having faith in a power greater than themselves (regardless of their religious views) gives them strength. During a particularly difficult time I wrote the following:

A Soft Reply

Divine Spirit, guide my way.
Lead, and I will follow you this day.

But soon my path, it grows so steep
As I watch the thistles grow and creep.

And thorns, they spread and block my way,
My soul and heart ache every day.

And, I cry.

This feels not right. Are you still there?
I can't feel you anywhere.

My tears flow, they blur my sight,
I am confused. What's wrong or right?

A gentle touch, a soft reply,
My tear is wiped from off my eye.

Have peace my child. Hear what I say.
I'm guiding you upon your way.

You do not need to search so far,
As you gaze upon that midnight star.

Just look and search within your soul.
For I am there, and you are whole.

What did I learn from my experiences and choices? Even though a judge eventually made me let them go, I learned that I would make the same choices all over again in welcoming my grandchildren into my home, loving them, and doing my best to raise them. I learned that all my efforts to help my grandchildren were not lost when they returned to their mother, something I had greatly feared. I learned that I regretted my lack of compassion and my judgmental attitude toward their parents. And I learned that love has no boundaries and with love, healing can happen.

PART TWO

Where to Start: What to Do and How to Do It

Legalities of Custody and Guardianship

I am always amazed at how many people email me and ask, "What are my rights as a grandparent and how do I get legal custody of my grandchild?" The first question is rather simple. You have no rights as a grandparent, other than those a judge gives you. A question I personally have is *when exactly did family members cease to have rights to a family child when a parent became unavailable to care for him? When did the government become responsible for decision-making versus the extended family? Was it in the 90's 80's, 70's, 60's, 50's, or earlier?* As I started to research the topic, I realized it would be a large project for a later time.

As for the second question about getting legal custody, I wish there was a simple answer, but it is never simple. There are various scenarios that will require different approaches. Not all cases will require the grandparent or relative to hire an attorney, but many will. In some states the proceedings are handled in the Probate Court and relatives are given guardianship of a child. In other states the proceedings are handled by the Juvenile and Domestic Relations Court and the relatives are given custody of a child. You will need to find out, either through a family law attorney or by calling the courthouse, how it works in your state. If you are pursuing custody or guardianship on your own – without the help of an attorney or social services – be prepared to provide proof that the parents are not responsible or are unable to care for their children for whatever reason. No court is going to give you custody of someone else's child just because you think you can do a better job or have a bigger house. I, personally, wouldn't even want it to be that easy. There must be ample evidence as to why the children should be with you. I had one grandmother write me, "I want to get custody of my grandbaby. My daughter is very neglectful. I want to adopt my grandchild because I am the one taking care for her." To that I merely asked, "Do you think the court would find her neglectful enough to take away her parental rights? She in fact has found a very competent caregiver - *you*. A judge may or may not consider that neglect." My point to the grandmother was not to discourage her from trying, but to help her realize that she may need more evidence than that. If a mother had plenty of money and hired a live-in nanny, she probably would not be viewed as neglectful. So, would she be viewed as neglectful simply because she was letting her mother care for the child fulltime? To take the scenario a bit further, if the mother was never available and the child needed medical care and couldn't receive it because the grandmother needed custody in order to obtain care, it may be viewed as neglect. I am not an attorney, but these are things to think about. By the way, the grandmother must not have liked my point because she never wrote me back.

In order to prove that a parent is unfit and that a relative should take legal custody of a child, evidence must be produced that supports the claim. That is, unless the parents willingly give legal custody to the relative. If the parents are not willing and the situation warrants it, keep a daily diary of everything that occurs – parental arrests, severe mental illness that incapacitates the parent, length of time parents disappear, drug and alcohol abuse - and all of the actions you are already taking to help the child. This is where good legal advice might be needed. If social services has already intervened and removed a child from his home, you may or may not need an attorney to present your case for gaining custody of the child.

The following are a few scenarios of real experiences that I have personally witnessed or been informed about by grandparents or relatives.

Case 1: A friend of mine hired an attorney. It might not have been necessary had she been willing to mire through all of the legal paperwork and had she been persistent, but the idea of doing it herself was overwhelming. The attorney did everything. She just showed up when he told her to. It was relatively easy, but expensive. The majority of grandparents that I know went this route. They hired an expensive attorney. Many borrowed from their retirement funds, put expenses on their credit cards, or even mortgaged their homes. The lucky ones had money in a simple savings account.

Case 2: A husband and wife accepted two little nephews into their home and were willing to raise them with their own children. They obtained the paperwork from the court house and proceeded on their own. Both parents were in prison. When presenting their paperwork to the court, they were told they had not done it right. The judge told them to come back after they had corrected the forms. They were frustrated, as he did not even tell them what needed correcting. They eventually received legal custody of the boys. Since the parents were going to be in prison for some time, the aunt and uncle wanted to adopt them. This proved more difficult than merely gaining custody. Since the unmarried, incarcerated parents were both against the idea, they were each awarded state-appointed attorneys to fight the process – paid for by the state. But the custodial aunt and uncle had to pay their own legal fees. I moved before I knew the outcome of the case.

Case 3: I knew an aunt who lived in Oregon. Her nephew had been in foster care for almost two years in another state on the east coast. When the court where the child lived was considering revoking the mother's parental rights, family members were contacted. The aunt was the only one in the family that was in a position to take the child. She flew to the custodial state, met with social services, went to court (without an attorney), went home, and proceeded to be cleared and approved through her own social services – doing everything she was told to do. The two states worked together with regards to the child's best welfare. The child was transferred from Virginia to Oregon under the care of the aunt. She would be his foster mother under the Oregon system for one year and then would legally adopt him. However, technically the child was adopted from Virginia. The aunt didn't know until the last minute whether the adoption would be considered a Virginia adoption or an Oregon adoption. It mattered because of any future benefits that might be available for the child. While the aunt did not have to fight anyone for custody, the child had spent almost two years in foster care before coming to her. During his foster care placement, he had little contact with his grandmother and other family members. When the state took the child into custody, family members were not allowed to have regular contact with him unless it had been pre-approved by the case worker and supervisor. Few phone calls were allowed, and gifts to the child had to be sent through DSS, unless given during an approved family visit. While this might be in the best interest for some children, it was not the best for this little boy. The entire family was grateful when the child was finally placed with his aunt. They could then have contact with him on a regular basis since he would now be raised as part of their extended family.

Case 4: A grandmother from the Midwest contacted me about her situation. She had actually become her grandchild's foster parent. That meant she had been trained by the state through their foster care program. She was technically her grandchild's foster mother and received the same financial payment as other foster parents did, which was typically much more than what a custodial grandparent received. However, while she received more financial assistance, she also did not have legal custody of the child; the state did. That meant the state made all important decisions and could remove the child from her care if and when they chose. She was the caregiver, but she had no legal rights to the child. Most states do not like to keep children in foster care for years. Not only is it very expensive to the state, but they want permanency for the child. In this case the state's ultimatum to the grandmother obviously had more to do with money than stability for the child. The state gave the grandmother a choice. She either had to adopt the child, thus receiving no further financial assistance because the child was no longer in the system, or the state would put the child up for adoption to nonfamily. The grandmother greatly needed the financial assistance and dreaded the anger that would come from the child's mother if she adopted the child. What was she to do? After a few emails were exchanged between us, we lost contact with each other. I can only surmise the grandmother chose to adopt her grandchild.

Case 5: In contrast to the above scenario, I was told by a grandmother in Texas that she was receiving foster care training through Foster Connections so she could be her grandchild's foster mother, while at the same time she was being given Permanent Managing Conservatorship (PMC). As the foster mother, she received a set monthly stipend and the child received Medicaid and would receive full college tuition if he attended college. This is because the child would technically stay in the foster care system his entire childhood while being raised by the grandmother. As the PMC for the child, the court would decide what rights and duties the grandmother would have awarded with regards to her grandchild.

Case 6: Late one night a grandmother received a call from a Sheriff's Deputy from another state. Could she come and get her three year old granddaughter? The child's parents had been arrested for serious crimes. The grandmother felt unprepared, but made the immediate choice to go and get her granddaughter. She then proceeded to obtain custody in her state. This grandmother was among the fortunate. The deputy could just as easily have called Child Protective Services, who could then have taken custody of the child and placed her in a temporary foster home without even telling the grandmother. The Fostering Connections Act (2009) mandates that child-welfare workers locate and contact relatives within 30 days of a child being removed from the custody of their parent(s). But, 30 days is a long time to a three year old. A different decision on the part of the police officer could have led to a drawn-out battle between the grandmother and the state where the child resided. However, even with this 2009 Act, how the law is interpreted varies from state to state. I know of one state who interpreted it as "If we believe you are a viable option for the child, we will contact you. Otherwise, we won't." Those were their words, without even knowing who the family members were. This agency felt no obligation to let this family know that a child in their family was even in the custody of the state.

These examples show the various confusing ways a grandparent or relative might become legally responsible to raise children that they had not expected to be raising. Some grandparents get children before they get put into the system and then have to legally fight to keep them. Others get the children from the system with encouragement and help, while others have to fight and, perhaps, take years to get children out of the foster care system. The trauma that can be done to these children is horrendous. If you choose to look into the possibility of becoming your grandchild's foster parent, thoroughly check with multiple people in your state to understand the benefits and risks.

Financial Resources

Frequently grandparents or other relatives write me wanting to know where they even start in finding resources for the extra children they are raising. There is no simple answer and, in some cases, practically no answers at all. In this section I am providing information that I have either experienced or have received from other grandparents throughout the United States. I have often found online information to be out of date or incorrect so double check everything you read.

Available resources for grandparents or other relative caregivers vary from state to state, county to county, and even community to community. Few areas seem to care when grandparents are merely babysitting their grandchildren, but when it comes to taking them to the doctor, enrolling them in school, or getting any financial assistance to help care for the children, that is another story. The best thing to do when searching for resources where you live is to find someone who has already been through it and find out what they did.

Places to start looking for any type of financial resource or support group would be:

- Local social services which might be called Department of Social Services (DSS), Department of Child and Family Services

(DCFS), Department of Human Services (DHS), Department of Family and Protective Services (DFPS), or maybe something else. Some people have had such awful experiences with their local social services that they don't want to contact them at all. At least call them for information, even if you don't tell them who you are.

- School guidance counselors are another resource who might know where you should start. Some people choose not to pursue any assistance because they do not want anyone from the system involved in their lives. I believe it unfortunate that so many people have had such horrible experiences that they would rather go without than risk government involvement. But, I clearly understand why they might feel that way.
- Local Area Agency on Aging may have some type of assistance for seniors over 60, but this is not always the case. Still, it is always a good idea to at least ask if they have or know of any programs geared toward seniors raising children.
- The local Health Department may have some services available needed by your grandchildren. More is written about this later in this chapter.
- Pediatricians or health facilities may have ideas about where to start in looking for services, but that may depend on how sympathetic their reception is to your cause. The idea is to contact anyone in your local area that deals with children and their various situations.
- Contact local churches to find out if they know of any support groups for grandparents raising children.
- Local food banks may be an option if you are in need of food.

When I lived in Virginia with my grandchildren and approached my local Department of Social Services (DSS), I had to first prove that the children were my grandchildren. I gathered together my birth certificate, my daughter's birth certificate, and the children's birth certificates. I was lucky I had all of them on hand. Then I collected my power of attorney (that my daughter provided for me) and all of our social security cards and took them to DSS. They walked me through the entire process and even helped me fill out the paperwork (They were a small group of friendly staff). The children received Medicaid, a child-only TANF grant (which amounted to about $290 for all three children), and free daycare through a licensed daycare provider. However, I soon discovered that other grandparents and family members in different counties in Virginia did not have it that easy. One grandmother was not able to receive even a child-only TANF grant because her daughter, the mother, had used up all of her TANF allotment. Eventually, the laws in Virginia were changed to allow the TANF benefits to follow the child. However, the new law only applied to grandparents whose grandchildren had already been taken by social services and put into the system, and DSS was placing them with the grandparent. This law did not apply to the majority of grandparents who had stepped in to help before the state took control. During a meeting I attended, I voiced my dislike for that new law. It helped only about 3% or 4% of custodial grandparents and children in the state of Virginia but was touted as a "great beginning." I thought it a very lousy beginning because I didn't see it as a beginning at all. Years later, it has still not been changed. While I personally do not believe that government programs can or even should attempt to solve all of our problems as custodial grandparents, I just did not like that the program was being heralded and praised as great progress when it wasn't.

In contrast to Virginia, one grandmother in Texas received a small Kinship assistance subsidy until she received permanent guardianship of her three grandchildren. At that point, her assistance stopped. The judge ordered the parents to pay child-support, but she rarely received any. Her husband was on social security and VA benefits, but for only the two of them since the boys were not adopted. Because his health was very poor and he was nearly blind, they received a small assistance from Adult Protective Services (APS). This assistance made them appear incompetent to care for children and they almost lost the children through Child Protective Services (CPS). Examples such as this make one hesitate to reach out and ask for help. Imagine the amount the state would have spent on putting three children in foster care, yet there was no financial help for these older grandparents. At some point, another of their daughters chose to drop off her six children at their house rather than have CPS get involved. The financial difficulties more than quadrupled. They did not know where to turn for help without running the risk of having the children farmed out through the foster care system.

In some states custodial grandparents receive financial assistance specifically designated for grandparents raising grandchildren, whether or not they have legal custody. It might sound like states such as these provide more assistance to relative caregivers. However, this might not be the case. Some states just label their financial assistance with different words. For example, in some states there are *state relative caregiver programs* where grandparents and relatives receive some financial assistance. However, this is not usually in addition to a child-only TANF grant. It is in place of it, and may not include any type of daycare assistance. Plus, in some states it may only be available to relatives where DCFS, DSS, DHS, or DFPS have already become involved and placed the children with that relative. The grandparents who rescued the child before the state got involved received no or very little help. Since agencies are called by different names in different states, you may need to find out what your local agency is called. School personnel or pediatricians should know. This can all be very confusing. That is why you will need to call your local agencies to find out what help your state has available for grandparents.

Another resource that may be available to grandparents with young children - infant through age four - is the Women, Infant, and Children (WIC) Supplemental Nutrition Program. This is usually run through the health department. It is a food program that provides formula, milk, juice, cereal, and other staple foods young children need. Proof is needed that you qualify. When I was benefitting from the program, the fact that the children were on Medicaid was sufficient proof. This program can be tremendously helpful in acquiring expensive baby formula and other foods for the children. One problem that many working grandmothers (and even mothers) have faced is that the WIC office is usually open only during normal working hours. Grandparents who work must take off work, often with no pay, which can pose extreme inconvenience and may make programs such as WIC an underutilized resource. Health departments may also provide needed vaccinations for children for free or at low cost. You may just find that you must ask for advice and referrals from anyone who might have any connections to anything.

In summary, start with calls to your grandchild's school guidance counselor, local social services, health department, pediatricians, health clinics, and any neighbor who may be utilizing any of these services. Ask them about:

- A child-only TANF grant or the equivalent
- WIC, food stamps
- Immunization clinics
- Medicaid or CHIP
- Daycare assistance
- Free or reduced school lunch or
- Any free or income based program available to help the children

If you are not used to having to ask for help, remember that this is for the children, and you most likely will need every possible resource that is available. Don't forget to ask about any community-based charity programs that are not government funded, such as food banks, churches who offer help to anyone in the community, utility assistance, help with school supplies, and even the Backpack Program - a program in some areas where organizations fill backpacks with food to be sent home with children for the weekend. Most grandparents or relatives raising children or single parents might benefit from any or all of these programs. However, if you don't need them, I would suggest that you not take advantage of them. Pass the information on to those who need it. If we assume others owe us because our life is difficult, we run the risk of losing a heart filled with gratitude.

It is important to remember that in some states, if you do not have legal custody or guardianship, there is no government financial assistance of any kind. As mentioned above in other states, assistance may end when you do gain legal guardianship. And be aware that, even if you do have legal custody and qualify to receive assistance, if the parent of your grandchild also lives with you or moves in with you later, you may no longer qualify for help from state or county agencies. This is determined according to state laws. It is important to investigate these issues in your state to avoid confusion or problems you had not anticipated.

Medical Care

Obtaining medical care for children is obviously very important. Most grandparents that have contacted me have Medicaid for the children or CHIP (Children Health Insurance Program). CHIP is low cost insurance for children who do not qualify for Medicaid. Still, I am continually appalled at the number of children who have no medical assistance at all. The social service department in your state (whatever it is called) should have information on qualifying the children for Medicaid or CHIP. An internet search is also a good way to learn how to apply and what to do. For example, if you want to learn about CHIP in Texas, Google *Texas CHIP* or for Medicaid, Google *Medicaid for children in Texas*. You will find a great deal of information, including how to apply online. When doing an internet search for any state in regards to Medicaid or CHIP, be careful that you first look at government sponsored websites. If you are uncertain, call the number on the website and ask them if they are a government-sponsored agency that can help you obtain Medicaid for your grandchildren. Some grandparents have been able to get their grandchild insured but not themselves, in spite of new health care laws. It may be necessary to find local health clinics who charge on a sliding fee. It may not be free, but it may be affordable.

School Enrollment

Depending on the state, school enrollment may not be an issue or it may seem like an insurmountable one if you do not have the exact paperwork they require. If possible, call your local school before the children arrive at your home and ask what is required to enroll your grandchildren. Some school systems may require nothing other than a statement that the children live with you. However, most states are not that simple. It often seems that they make it as difficult as possible. Be prepared to provide:

- A court order to prove legal guardianship of the child, or a power of attorney if they will accept that
- A certified copy of the child's birth certificate
- The child's social security card
- Proof that you live in the school's district

In the county where I lived, they accepted my power of attorney for my legal document. However, that didn't work for another grandmother who lived in a nearby county in my same state. She had lived in that same county for several years - paying school taxes – but could not enroll her grandchildren in school until a judge awarded her temporary custody and she had the order to prove it. This was frustrating and very stressful for her. Even parents can have challenges enrolling their own children if there has been a change in the custody arrangement. One mother I know regained custody of her children but lost the custody order during the process of moving to another state. Had the school known of the custody history, she (even as the mother) would have been faced with *prove you have legal custody*. Instead she went to the school with birth certificates, social security cards, and proof of residence and simply did not mention the prior custody issue or that it could appear confusing when the old school records finally arrived. Fortunately, the children were enrolled without a hitch. Unfortunately, enrolling children in school does not usually happen that easily for the grandparent.

For clarity, first call the schools and ask what they require for enrollment by a grandparent or relative. Prepare early by obtaining birth certificates and social security cards. Keep them together with any legal documents you have pertaining to custody issues. I know of a family that let their teenage niece live with them. They were not pursuing custody because they did not expect her to stay with them for more than a school year. The mother of the child (who did not live with them) went to the school with the aunt and enrolled the child in school, stating that they all lived with the aunt. After the child was enrolled, the mother left to *get her life together*, which she successfully did. The next year the child returned to her mother. This family simply had to subvert the rules. By state law, the child had to be in school, but by state law the aunt could not enroll her without having legal custody. They had little choice but to have the mother enroll the girl, even though the mother did not live with the family. I am continually amazed at how difficult some states make it to simply take care of your own family.

In Utah, I have known of easier situations. An aunt went to the school with her niece and a power of attorney from the out-of-state mother. She had no problem enrolling her niece in school. Another grandmother simply went to the school and stated that the grandchild lived with her. Again, she had no difficulty. Of course, laws seem to change regularly, so there is no guarantee it would be still that easy for you in Utah. To avoid unneeded frustration, call the school first and ask what they need.

Internet Resources

The following websites will get you started on your search for information about raising your grandchildren. Some of these websites will provide general information, while others may provide information more specific to where you live. When doing a general Internet search in your favorite search engine, type in the name of your *state* (or country if not in the United States) along with specific phrases such as: *grandparents raising grandchildren, custody of grandchildren, adopting grandchildren, kinship care.* For example, if you live in Texas, search *grandparents raising grandchildren in Texas.*

Raising Your Grandchildren (*RaisingYourGrandchildren.com*) is a website developed and maintained by Karen Best Wright to help grandparents and relatives raising children find available resources and information. (This is my personal website. I make every effort to keep it updated with current information.) Click on the *State Resources* link to find information pertinent to your state or on the *Internet Resources* link for general online resources relating to kinship care.

Grandparenting Blog (www.GrandparentingBlog.com (needs the www. in front) is my personal blog for grandparents and relatives raising children.

Generations United (www.gu.org) supports the development and expansion of programs bringing children, youth, and older adults together.

National Kinship Alliance for Children (www.KinshipAllience. org) is a nationwide network of grandparents, community members, and professionals working together to provide education and support, advocacy, and thought leadership for children, grandparents, and kinship families. This website has some excellent information.

AARP (American Association of Retired Persons) (www.AARP.com) provides a wide range of services and information for American seniors. When looking for information on their website for grandparents, type inside AARP's own website's search box the words *grandparents raising grandchildren.*

GRAND (www.grandmagazine.com) is an online magazine filled with helpful information and articles for grandparents or relatives raising children.

The Addict's Mom g2g (Grandparent to Grandparent). This Facebook page is a closed forum. You need to make a request to become a member. This is a place for grandparents to share without shame. (https://www.facebook.com/groups/154033158118579/)

CANGRANDS (www.CanGrands.com) is a not-for-profit organization devoted to providing kinship support for caregiver families across Canada.

Grandparents Raising Grandchildren in Australia. (*www.raisinggrandchildren.com.au*)

The Grandparents' Association_in the UK. (*www.grandparents-association.org.uk*)

Raising Grandchildren in New Zealand, (*www.raisinggrandchildren.net.nz*)

APPENDIX

Kinship Care Wellness Assessment

This assessment focuses on six aspects of health and wellness: Physical – Emotional - Mental/ Intellectual – Social – Spiritual - Environmental.

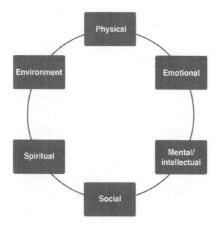

For the purpose of this assessment, health is defined as a state of being. Wellness is defined here as dynamic, the process of living a healthy lifestyle. This assessment is designed to help you empower yourself and your grandchildren to improve your lifestyle. Note that when using the words *grandchildren* and *grandparent*, these words apply to all kinship relationships. If you are a different relative, mentally substitute your title for *grandparent*. For each section below, circle the number to the left that applies for each row. You may want to photocopy the wellness assessment for your own multiple uses or use a spiral notebook or journal in which to record your answers.

Physical Health and Wellness

What are your greatest personal health concerns? Choose all that apply.

Weight ◊ High Blood Pressure ◊ High Cholesterol ◊ Diabetes ◊ Arthritis ◊ Allergies ◊ Fatigue ◊ Stress ◊ Depression ◊ Anxiety ◊ Headaches ◊ Chronic Pain ◊ Other ◊

OVER-ALL HEALTH

How many health concerns do you have?

1   health concern
2   health concern
3   health concern
4   health concern
5   5 or more health concerns

How do you consider your health as the grandparent?

1   excellent
2   above average
3   average
4   poor
5   very poor

What are your exercise habits? (Includes walking for fitness, aerobics, weight lifting, dancing, etc.)

1   exercise daily
2   exercise at least 3 times a week
3   exercise once a week
4   exercise less than once a week
5   rarely exercise

What type of foods do you eat daily? (Processed foods are foods from a box or can.)

1   Fresh vegetables and fruits and low fat meat or plant protein daily
2   Combination of fresh vegetables, fruits, fried food, and processed foods, no daily high sugar foods.
3   Combination of fresh vegetables, fruits, fried food, and processed foods, daily high sugar foods.
4   Mostly high sugar, high fat, fried foods, and/or processed foods daily
5   Only high sugar, high fat, fried foods, and/or processed foods daily

What are your smoking habits?

1   I do not smoke
2   I smoke occasionally (i.e. at a party)
3   I smoke daily (lightly)
4   I smoke daily (moderately)
5   I smoke daily (heavy)

Total points for physical wellness _____ (the higher the number, the higher the risk)

Strengths and Weaknesses for Physical Wellness

a. What do you consider your greatest strengths in regards to your physical wellness

b. What do you think needs to change in your physical wellness?

Emotional Health and Wellness

How one handles stress, relationships, depression, and challenges.

How is your general sense of well-being?

1   Upbeat and positive most of the time
2   Have my ups and downs, which seem normal
3   Feel down and depressed more than I like
4   Overwhelmed and depressed often
5   Overwhelmed and depressed all of the time

How do you consider your organizational skills (time management, housekeeping, etc.)?

1   Very organized and in control of my life
2   Quite organized and am satisfied
3   Not as organized as I would like but okay
4   Unorganized and need to improve
5   Terribly unorganized and out of control

How well do you handle grief and loss in your life?

1   Satisfied with how I handle grief and loss
2   Not satisfied but things are okay
3   Need to improve
4   Damaging my life
5   Helpless in dealing with grief and loss

In general, how do you feel about your relationships with others?

1   Very satisfied with my relationships
2   Dissatisfied but feel things are okay
3   Stressful and need to improve
4   Very stressful and are damaging my life
5   Unable to cope with relationships in my life

How do you feel about your ability to handle the stress in your life?

1   Pleased with how I handle stress
2   Satisfied with how I handle stress
3   Dissatisfied, but things are in control
4   Damaging my life, working on it
5   Damaged, helpless, need help

Total points for emotional wellness _____ (the higher the number, the higher the risk)

Strengths and Weaknesses for Emotional Wellness

a. What do you consider your greatest strengths in regards to emotional wellness?

b. What needs to change in your emotional wellness?

Mental / Intellectual Health and Wellness

Mental activities, decision making, and thinking skills

How satisfied are you with your reading and writing skills?

1   Very satisfied, at advanced level
2   Not advanced but feel no need to improve
3   Okay but would like to improve
4   Dissatisfied with reading and writing skills, like to improve
5   Read and write English poorly

How satisfied are you with your ability to learn a new skill (i.e. computer use)?

1   Learn new skills easily
2   Learn new skills but with effort
3   Difficult to learn new skills, but I manage
4   Difficult to learn new skills, need help
5   Too Difficult to even try and learn new skills

How satisfied are you with your ability to concentrate?

1   Very, no problems with concentrating
2   Not satisfied but okay
3   Want my concentration ability to improve
4   Struggle but don't really care
5   Can't focus and concentrate at all, real problem

How satisfied are you with your ability to make decisions?

1 Very satisfied
2 Somewhat satisfied, no major problems
3 Unsatisfied but I manage
4 Make decision but can't follow through
5 Very dissatisfied and need help

How satisfied are you with your memory?

1 Excellent memory
2 Memory not great but okay
3 Memory poor, write notes to myself
4 Memory poor and forget many things
5 Memory very poor, might have a real health problem

Total points for mental/intellectual wellness ___ (the higher the number, the higher the risk)

Strengths and Weaknesses for Intellectual Wellness

a. What do you consider your greatest strengths in regards to your mental/intellectual wellness?

b. What do you want to change in regards to your mental/intellectual wellness?

Social Health and Wellness

Social Wellness has to do with your relationships with other people, both within your close circle of family and friends and others in society.

How satisfied are you with family members you live with?

    1   Satisfied and happy
    2   Happy with some but not others
    3   Not happy but working on it
    4   Overwhelmed but getting help
    5   Overwhelmed and not getting help

How satisfied are you with your relationship with your grandchildren's parents?

    1   Very satisfied and happy
    2   Does not affect me either way
    3   Dissatisfied but managing
    4   Dissatisfied but getting help
    5   Very dissatisfied, awful

How satisfied are you with your relationship with friends?

    1   Very satisfied, have great friends
    2   Somewhat satisfied, okay
    3   Dissatisfied, friends really don't understand
    4   Dissatisfied, friends don't really care
    5   Dissatisfied, have no friends, need friends

How satisfied are you with your connection to your community (church, neighborhood, support groups, etc.)

1   Very satisfied, great community
2   Marginal support in my community
3   Looking for a support system, optimistic
4   Looking for a support system, discouraged
5   Dissatisfied, no support system at all.

How satisfied are you with your fun social life?

1   Very satisfied, fun social life
2   Satisfied even with no fun social life
3   Dissatisfied, looking for more fun
4   Dissatisfied, nothing feels fun
5   Very withdrawn, don't care anymore

Total points for social wellness ____ (the higher the number, the higher the risk)

Strengths and Weaknesses for Social Wellness

a.   What do you consider your greatest strengths in regards to your social wellness?

b.   What do you want to change in regards to your social wellness?

Spiritual Health and Wellness

Spirituality is defined here as your relationship with God or a higher power, or your sense of purpose in your life.

How satisfied are you with the level of spirituality in your life?

1   Very satisfied with my spirituality
2   Somewhat satisfied but could be better
3   Dissatisfied, need spiritual outlook
4   Dissatisfied, discouraged
5   Feel no spirituality or purpose to my life

How satisfied are you when you pray or contemplate in a positive way about your spirituality?

1   Very satisfied
2   Somewhat satisfied but could improve
3   Dissatisfied but am working on it
4   Dissatisfied, difficulty with prayer or contemplation in a positive way
5   Dissatisfied, don't even try

How satisfied are you with how you receive personal spiritual guidance (from a pastor, helpful books, or receiving direction directly from God or your belief in a divine power).

1   Very satisfied
2   Somewhat satisfied
3   Dissatisfied but working on it
4   Dissatisfied and discouraged
5   Dissatisfied, don't even try

How often do you receive spiritual guidance (prayer, books, pastor, positive thoughts, etc.)?

1 Multiple times a day
2 Daily
3 Weekly
4 Occasionally
5 Don't try, feel hopeless

How satisfied are you with your spiritual connection to others?

1 Very satisfied
2 Somewhat satisfied
3 Dissatisfied but feel positive anyway
4 Dissatisfied, frustrated and lonely
5 Dissatisfied, don't even try anymore

Total points for spiritual wellness ____ (the higher the number, the higher the risk)

Strengths and Weaknesses for Spiritual Wellness

a. What do you consider your greatest strengths in regards to your spiritual wellness?

b. What do you want to change in regards to your spiritual wellness?

Environmental Health and Wellness

For the purpose of this assessment, environmental wellness refers to your home environment, work environment, and neighborhood environment (not the world environment).

How satisfied are you with the physical environment of your home.

1   Very satisfied – clean, adequate, safe
2   Somewhat satisfied, want it better
3   Dissatisfied, working on improvements
4   Dissatisfied, need help with improvements
5   Dissatisfied, need a different place to live

How satisfied are you with the emotional environment of your home?

1   Very satisfied, love, laughter, fun, happy
2   Satisfied, emotions seem normal
3   Dissatisfied, anger, sadness, working on it
4   Dissatisfied, anger, sadness, need help
5   Dissatisfied, anger, sadness, unbearable

How do you consider your work environment (physical)?

1   Great, clean and safe
2   Sometimes clean and safe but not always
3   Often feel unsafe and dirty, but improving
4   Feels unsafe and dirty most of the time
5   Work environment dangerous

How do you consider your work environment (emotionally)?

1   Great, friendly, positive, healthy
2   Sometimes good but not always
3   Neutral, no problems either way
4   Not good, anger, criticism, negativity
5   Very bad, highly stressful and negative

How do you consider your neighborhood/community environment?

1   Clean and safe, can walk freely at night
2   Clean and safe, walk around only in daylight
3   Mostly safe but am cautious
4   Mostly unsafe, always cautious
5   Not safe, high crime, traffic, violence

Total points for environmental wellness ____ (the higher the number, the higher the risk)

Strengths / Weaknesses for Environmental Wellness

a.   What do you consider your greatest strengths in regards to your environmental wellness?

b.   What do you want to change in your environment?

Kinship Care Wellness Assessment

Total high-risk points

Physical _____

Emotional_____

Mental/Intellectual_____

Social_____

Spiritual_____

Environmental_____

Areas of Greatest Strengths

_____

_____

_____

Areas that Need Improvement

_____

_____

_____

Personal Goal Setting

Setting goals does not need to be complicated and can actually be fun, with the support and encouragement of others. This program is designed to help you set your own goals to help you improve your own life through creating your own "Be Goals" and "Do Goals."

"Be Goals"

"Be Goals" are the types of goals that refer to what you want "To Be." For example, as a kinship care provider, you may want "to be" healthy, financially stable, a loving or patient grandparent, organized, emotionally or spiritually strong, socially well-adjusted (friendly), knowledgeable about nutrition, or even better educated. "Be Goals" are broad, with a large m of something you want to accomplish or be.

"Do Goals"

"Do Goals" are things you might choose to do to accomplish your "Be Goal." For example, a caregiver who wants to be healthy might choose from a variety of things "to do," such as eat less fat and sugar, start a walking program, or get better sleep. A person who wants to be financially stable might choose to learn how to budget money better, find available resources, or learn a new skill to help earn additional money. Likewise, a person who wants to be emotionally stronger might choose to seek support through friends or a church, accept counseling, or learn stress management skills.

How to Start

First, start with one "Be Goal." What broad picture of yourself can you imagine? After deciding on one thing you want to improve or accomplish, select at least one thing you can do to help yourself achieve that goal. Select something within your control. For example, if you want to manage stress better, you would choose an activity you could do such as go to bed earlier or learn how to relax better. You would not make a choice for your grown child to change their behavior to make your life easier. You do not have control over someone else's choices, only your own. So, let's start.

Setting Your New Goal

Example 1: **Person A** wants to be healthier by controlling diabetes. That is the "be goal." The "do goal" might be to reduce sugar and fat intake. Some helpful ideas might be to learn which foods you should eat or not eat, learn how to keep a food diary, learn how to read food labels, and learn where you can get this information.

Example 2: **Person B** wants to be more energetic (the "be goal"). The "do goal" might be to get more sleep. Some ideas that may help you might be to talk to your doctor, monitor your evening activities to learn what overstimulates you, or watch what you are eating late at night.

Select One "Be Goal"

Select at least one "Do Goal"

What ideas can help you with your "Do Goal?"